G000122682

# BRADSHAW'S GUIDE TO SCOTLAND'S RAILWAYS PART 1:

## CARLISLE TO INVERNESS

Campbell McCutcheon

AMBERLEY PUBLISHING

Fond Delusion
*First Tourist (going North).* 'Hullo, Tompk—"

*Second Tourist (ditto).* 'Hsh—sh! Confound it, you'll spoil all. They think in the train I'm a Highland chief!

## About this book

*Bradshaw's Guide* explores many aspects of the railway journeys to be had on Scotland's railways. Through Bradshaw's text and the supportive images, the lines are described, and main features shown. Of course, some of the lines have been closed and others have opened since Bradshaw compiled this guide in 1863. Hopefully, it will encourage you to delve into the history of the railways of the west of Scotland and encourage you to visit some otherwise bypassed town. Please note that public access to railway lines is restricted for reasons of safety.

First published 2014

Amberley Publishing
The Hill, Stroud
Gloucestershire, GL5 4EP

www.amberley-books.com

Copyright © Campbell McCutcheon and John Christopher , 2014

The right of Campbell McCutcheon and John Christopher to be identified as the Author of this work has been asserted in accordance with the Copyrights, Designs and Patents Act 1988.

ISBN 978 1 4456 3393 0
E book ISBN 978 14456 3404 3

British Library Cataloguing in Publication Data. A catalogue record for this book is available from the British Library.

Typeset in 9.5pt on 12pt Celeste.
Typesetting by Amberley Publishing.
Printed in the UK.

# Bradshaw on Scotland

A haggis is a pudding exclusively Scotch, but considered of French origin. Its ingredients are oatmeal, suet, pepper, &c., and it is usually boiled in a sheep's stomach. Although a heavy, yet it is by no means a disagreeable dish.

Bradshaw's vivid and obviously agreeable description of the haggis is just one of the interesting anecdotes and descriptions that lift *Bradshaw's Descriptive Railway Hand-Book of Great Britain and Ireland* from a tome describing the railway routes in existence north of the border in 1863 to a genuine informative guidebook of the most important places in Scotland. This book is one of a series published by Amberley which helps bring Bradshaw into the twenty-first century, giving the reader a font that is readable and a breadth of illustrative material that help to portray the Scotland that the Bradshaw's Guide writers would have seen on their travels in 1861–63 as they compiled the guide. Two parts will bring the Scotland of the 1860s to life, with this, the first, primarily concerning itself with the west coast and Highlands, and part two covering what we now know as the East Coast Main Line and the railways of eastern Scotland. Ultimately, the series, which already covers the lines of Isambard Kingdom Brunel, the Great Western Railway and the South East of England, will encompass all of the railways of the United Kingdom and of Ireland.

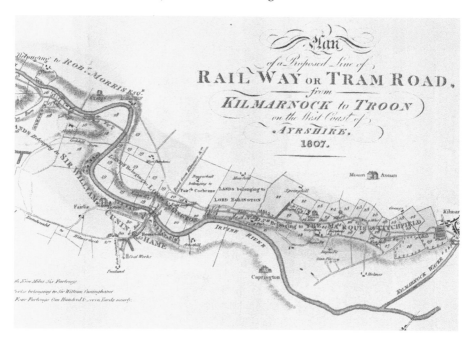

## Bradshaw and Scotland

George Bradshaw was born in 1801 and died in 1853 at the age of fifty-two. His publishing empire had begun in the canal age, and he produced a series of maps and guides of Britain's canals. With the advent of the railways, his attention turned to guides to the new form of transport and, by 1863, his guide covered the whole of the United Kingdom. Scotland itself had some of Britain's oldest railways, from the KIlmarnock & Troon to the Garnkirk & Glasgow. The Kilmarnock & Troon was one of the pioneer railways to operate a locomotive hauled service, predating both the Stockton & Darlington and the Liverpool & Manchester Railways. By the 1860s, mineral rich Scotland was criss-crossed by railway routes, with lines branching into the Highlands, as well as to the main ferry ports on the west coast. Still to come were such engineering marvels as the Tay and Forth railway bridges, although the Royal Border Bridge at Berwick-upon-Tweed had already opened, completing the route from Newcastle to Edinburgh.

It is fair to say that the railways are the Victorians' greatest legacy to the twentieth and twenty-first centuries. They shrank space and time. Before their coming different parts of the country had existed in local time based on the position of the sun, with Bristol, for example, running ten minutes behind London. The Great Western Railway changed all that in 1840 when it applied synchronised railway time throughout its area. The presence of the railways defined the shape and development of many of our towns and cities, they altered the distribution of the population and forever changed the fundamental patterns of our lives. For many millions of Britons the daily business of where they live and work, and travel between the two, is defined by the network of iron rails laid down nearly two centuries ago by the engineers and an anonymous army of railway navvies.

The timing of the publication of Bradshaw's guidebooks is interesting. This particular account is taken from the 1863 edition of the handbook although, for practical reasons, it must have been written slightly earlier, probably between 1860 and 1862. By this stage the railways had lost their pioneering status, and with the heady days of the railway mania of the 1840s over they were settling into the daily business of transporting people and goods. By the early 1860s the main line from Glasgow to Edinburgh, for example, had been in operation for around fifteen years but the large bridges spanning the Forth and the Tay were still a good fifteen–thirty years away, while the lines to the Western Highlands were still to be proposed and constructed. It was also by this time that rail travel had become sufficiently commonplace to create a market for Bradshaw's guides.

As a young man George Bradshaw had been apprenticed to an engraver in Manchester in 1820, and after a spell in Belfast he returned to Manchester to set up his own business as an engraver and printer specialising principally in maps. In October 1839 he produced the world's first compilation of railway timetables. Entitled *Bradshaw's Railway Time Tables and Assistant to Railway Travelling*, the slender cloth-bound volume sold for sixpence. By 1840 the title had changed to *Bradshaw's Railway*

*Companion* and the price doubled to one shilling. It then evolved into a monthly publication with the price reduced to the original and more affordable sixpence.

Although George Bradshaw died in 1853 the company continued to produce the monthly guides and in 1863 it launched Bradshaw's *Descriptive Railway Hand-Book of Great Britain and Ireland* (which forms the basis of this series of books). It was originally published in four sections as proper guidebooks without any of the timetable information of the monthly publications. Universally referred to as Bradshaw's Guide it was this guidebook that features in Michael Portillo's *Great British Railway Journeys,* and as a result of its exposure to a new audience the book found itself catapulted into the best-seller list almost 150 years after it was originally published.

Without a doubt the Bradshaw Guides were invaluable in their time and they provide the modern-day reader with a fascinating insight into the mid-Victorian rail traveller's experience. In 1865 *Punch* had praised Bradshaw's publications, stating that 'seldom has the gigantic intellect of man been employed upon a work of greater utility'. Having said that, the usual facsimile editions available nowadays don't make especially easy reading with their columns of close-set type. There are scarcely any illustrations for a start, and attempts to trace linear journeys from A to B are interrupted by distracting branch line diversions. That's where this volume comes into its own. *Bradshaw's Guide to Scotland's Railways, Volume 1,* takes the reader on a continuous journey from the border at Carlisle via the Glasgow & South Western routes into Dumfries and Galloway all the way to the furthest northern extent of the railways of 1863, at Dingwall. The illustrations show scenes from Victorian times and they are juxtaposed with photographs of the locations as they are today. The accompanying information provide greater background detail on the sights to be seen, the railways and the many locations along the route.

## The railways

In 1863, the major railway amalgamations that took place in Scotland were still two years away. The main five railway lines that would operate into the 1920s (Glasgow & South Western, Caledonian, North British, Great North of Scotland and Highland) were in existence but the Scottish Central, Inverness & Aberdeen, Edinburgh & Glasgow and numerous other independent companies still existed, breaking up the major routes into smaller sections. On the West Coast route to Aberdeen, one would traverse some three or four different companies' lines and the East Coast route was no better, but this time the route was broken by the Firths of Forth and Tay, with ferries operating to Fife from both Granton and Dundee.

The journey begins with the line from Carlisle to Glasgow via Dumfries and the branches from it. This was Glasgow & South Western territory and it encompassed the Irish Sea port of Portpatrick, the mineral-rich county of Ayrshire and the Clyde Coast towns of Renfrewshire. Included were the burgeoning port towns of Greenock and Port Glasgow, with their numerous shipyards. The route via Dumfries gave an

GLASGOW | EDINBURGH

by | by

"THE CORONATION SCOT" | "THE CORONATION"

Euston · Glasgow in 6½ hours | King's Cross · Edinburgh in 6 hours

| | | | | |
|---|---|---|---|---|
| MONDAYS TO FRIDAYS | | | MONDAYS TO FRIDAYS | |
| EUSTON | dep. 1·30 p.m. | | KING'S CROSS | dep. 4·0 p.m. |
| GLASGOW (CENTRAL) | arr. 8·0 p.m. | | EDINBURGH (WAVERLEY) | arr. 10·0 p.m. |
| GLASGOW (CENTRAL) | dep. 1·30 p.m. | | EDINBURGH (WAVERLEY) | dep. 4·30 p.m. |
| EUSTON | arr. 8·0 p.m. | | KING'S CROSS | arr. 10·30 p.m. |

LONDON MIDLAND AND SCOTTISH RAILWAY | LONDON AND NORTH EASTERN RAILWAY

THE FIRST "BRADSHAW"
A reminiscence of Whitsun Holidays in Ancient Egypt. From an old-time tabl(e)ature

alternative to the Caledonian main line from Carlisle to Glasgow via Beattock and the industrial belt of Lanarkshire.

From Carlisle, we also traverse the Caledonian main line and its branches, all the way north to Stirling, where the Scottish Central Railway took over, and where minor lines such as the now-defunct Forth & Clyde Junction Railway (operated by the North British) into the Dunbartonshire industrial towns of Alexandria and the Vale of Leven, and the Stirling & Dunfermline route into Fife terminated.

The lines of Perthshire and the Highlands are covered in later sections of this book and for the most part they were branches, except for the main line to Inverness and the routes to Aberdeen from both Inverness and Perth. The original route of the Highland is covered as the short cut near Aviemore had yet to be built. At the time of publication, in 1863, the railway stopped at Invergordon, a good harbour, on the north side of the Cromarty Firth. This volume covers the West of Scotland and the Highlands, with the next volume of Bradshaw's Guide covering the Borders, East Coast, Fife and the North East of Scotland. Enjoy this journey on the railways of 1863.

*Opposite, top left:* George Bradshaw.

*Opposite, top right:* An advertising poster for the streamlined expresses on the East and West Coast main lines.

*Opposite:* Scotland was famed for its innovative railways, from the first electric train on the Edinburgh-Glasgow line to the George Bennie railplane at Milngavie.

*Right:* The first train of the Glasgow & Garnkirk Railway arrives at St Rollox, Glasgow, 1831.

*Clockwise from top left:*
Caledonian Railway 4-6-0
at Annan, *c.* 1925.

The Tri-jubilee of Robert
Burns' birth at his
mausoleum in Dumfries.

The White Sands at
Dumfries, *c.* 1890.

Glasgow & South Western
Railway tank loco No.1.

# Glasgow & South Western

## Carlisle to Kilmarnock
Gretna Green – See page 41.

### ANNAN
A telegraph station.

HOTEL – Queensberry Arms.

MARKET DAY – Thursday.

FAIRS – 1st Thursday in May and 3rd Thursday in October.

This is a royal and parliamentary burgh, with a population of about 4,670, who return one member, jointly with Dumfries, and are engaged in the coasting and shipbuilding trades, salmon fisheries, and gingham factories; contains three chapels, town house, market place, cotton mill, rope houses, three schools, and two churches, the oldest of which has a fine spire, Dr. Blackleek, the blind poet, and the late Edward Irving, were natives.

Next follows the station of CUMMERTREES, which takes its name from 'Curmshir-tree' (Long Valley Town), near which lies Hoddam Castle, seat of General Sharpe, built by Lord Herries, under a hill on which is placed a Beacon, called the Tower of Repentance, about 20 feet high; and five miles further on we pass RUTHWELL station, close to which are Comlongan Castle, an old seat of the Earl of Mansfield. The church is ancient, and formerly contained the figured runic pilar, 18 feet high, which was moved to the manse in 1644. Cockpool, which belonged to the Murras and Kirkstyles, which the Knights Templars held.

### DUMFRIES
A telegraph station.

HOTELS – King's Arms, Commercial.

MARKET DAY – Wednesday and Saturday.

FAIRS – Every Wednesday in January, February, March, and December, last Wednesday in April, Wednesday before the 26th May, Wednesday after June 17th, September 25th, or Wednesday after 3rd Wednesday in October, Wednesday before and after November 22nd.

BANKERS – British Linen Co.; Commercial Bank of Scotland; Bank of Scotland; National Bank of Scotland; Western Bank of Scotland; Edinburgh and Glasgow Bank.

At the Commercial Inn, Charles Stuart took up his head quarters, in 1745.

*Crichton Royal Institution (First House), Dumfries.*

*Clockwise from top left:* A Pullman train at Dumfries station en route for St Enoch.

Dalbeattie harbour, with a sailing ship laden with granite.

Dumfries High Street with the fountain and midsteeple, built in 1705–7.

Bradshaw mentions Dr Crichton's Lunatic Asylum.

A Scottish royal and parliamentary burgh (one member), and the capital of Dumfriesshire, on the river Nith, near the Solway Frith. Population about 13,166. It has a little shipping trade; shoes and cotton goods are the principal manufactures. The site is flat and mossy, but the soil fertile, with the Nithsdale Hills in the distance. The streets are clean and well built. Pleasant walks line the river's bank. Three slender spires are the first to strike the stranger's eye; one belongs to St. Michael's, an old church of the 13th century, containing, it is calculated, in and about it, above 1,800 monuments of all kinds. In the corner of the churchyard is the handsome mausoleum to Burns, set up by subscription, in 1815. A beaten path made by thousands of visitors strikes across the other graves. Within the church is an emblematic piece or marble, by Turnerelli, to the memory of the poet, who lived here as an exciseman from 1791 to his death in 1796. His widow survived him till 1834, living at a small house in Burns-Street.

Here are a Court House, Academy, a Pillar to the excellent Duke of Queensberry, Dr. Crichton's Lunatic Asylum; and an old bridge, built by Baliol's mother, Devergilla, who also founded the Greyfriars, in which Bruce killed the Red Comyn, in 1305. Kean made his first appearance in the Dumfries Theatre. Excellent bacon and hams are cured here, and vast numbers of small cattle pass this way to be fattened for market in Norfolk and Essex. Bruce was Lord of Annandale, a district in this neighbourhood, where many events of his early life took place.

On the opposite side of the Nith is Lincluden Castle. Further south you come to Caerlaverock Castle, the original of 'Elangowan' in Scott's *Guy Mannering*, the scenery of which, and of *Red Gauntlet*, are described from this part of Scotland.

At Tinwald, on the hills (near the old Watling street), Patterson, the founder of the Bank of England, was born.

## CASTLE DOUGLAS AND DUMFRIES

Leaving Dumfries we immediately cross the river Nith, famous for its trout and salmon, pass the stations of MAXWELLTOWN, LOCHANHEAD, and KILLNWHAN, and arrive at

KIRKGUNZEON, a little village in the centre of a hilly grazing district. In the vicinity are the remains of three Roman Camps.

SOUTHWICK station.

DALBEATTIE, a small stone-built town with a population of about 1,500, engaged in shipping.

## CASTLE DOUGLAS

A telegraph station.

MARKET DAY – Monday.

This is a town of growing importance with a population of about 2,000, and situated about a mile and a half to the south of Carlingwark Loch, a large sheet of water, abounding with perch, &c. It has also several small well-wooded islands. Thrieve Castle, formerly belonging to the Douglasses, is situate a little to the west of the town, on a little island in the Dee. Its remains date from the fourteenth century.

Near Kirkcudbright, they profess to show, at Rueberry, Dirk Hatteraick's Cave, and the Gauger's Loup, where poor Frank Kennedy was thrown over by the smugglers.

## PORTPATRICK
CROSSMICHAEL and PARTON stations.
NEW GALLOWAY (a telegraph station), situate on the river Ken, which at this point widens very considerably, which circumstance, together with the bold and picturesque aspect of the scenery along its banks, render it a place of considerable interest to the tourist.

CREETOWN station.

## NEWTON STEWART
A telegraph station.
MARKET DAY – Friday.
FAIRS are held on the second Friday in each month, also on the last Wednesday in April, July, and October.

This town has a population of about 2,600, engaged in the manufacture of leather. It is situated on the river Cree, which here forms the boundary line between the counties of Kirkcudbright and Wigtown. The bridge across the river is a noble structure.

KIRKCOWAN and GLENLUCE station.

## STRANRAER
A telegraph station.
MARKET DAY – Friday.
It is a seaport town at the top of Loch Ryan, accessible to steamers of heavy tonnage. The town itself has no particular attraction, but the country around is very interesting. Its position however can hardly be overestimated as forming the most expeditious route from Scotland to Ireland, in connection with the Belfast and Northern Counties at Larne. There is daily and daylight service performed, the Channel sailing being only two hours, and Loch sailing 45 minutes.

Kennedy Castle, 3 ½ miles to the east of the town, once the residence of the Earls of Cassills, was destroyed by fire in 1715. A part of the walls are still remaining, and the grounds are kept in excellent condition.

COLFIN STATION

PORTPATRICK
A small village, the inhabitants of which are generally engaged either in fishing or weaving. It is situated on a very rocky coast, and commands extensive sea views.

HOLYWOOD and AULDGIRTH stations.

CLOSEBURN
   Telegraph station at Thornhill, 2 ¾ miles.
   MONEY ORDER OFFICE at Thornhill, 2 ¾ miles.
Here are the ruins of an old castle of the Kilpatricks, Closeburn Hall, seat of Sir J. S. Menteith, Bart., and at Crichup Linn, a fall of 90 feet, was Balfour of Burley's Cave, the retreat of the persecuted covenanters.
THORNHILL and CARRON BRIDGE stations.

SANQUHAR
   A telegraph station.
   HOTELS – Fergusson's.
   MARKET DAY – Saturday.
   FAIRS – 1st Friday in February, 3rd Friday in April, 1st Friday in May, Friday before 17th July, 1st Friday in November.
   BANKERS – British Linen Company; Western Bank of Scotland.

KIRKCONNEL – The church here has an antique square tower. The 'admirable Crichton' was born at Elliock House. In the vicinity are Castle Gilmour, a moot hill, and ruins of a hospital.

AYRSHIRE
This county, which returns one member, is in the shape of two wings, extending to the north-west and south-west, and forming a vast bay at the mouth of the Firth of Clyde, and has abundant mines of coal; also freestone, limestone, iron, lead, and copper; and from the great abundance of sea-weed which is cast ashore, vast quantities of kelp is made. Ayrshire is called the 'Land of Burns', who was born near the town of Ayr, and interred in Dumfries, where a monument was erected to his memory. But the most interesting cenotaph of Burns, which so many travellers visit, is that at Alloway, situated in most beautiful and romantic scenery, in the native parish of the poet, near the Auld Brig O' Doon, and 'Alloway's auld hanted Kirk,' through one of the windows of which Tam O' Shanter saw

*Above:* The Stranraer boat train of the Glasgow & South Western Railway. With its sheltered loch, Stranraer provided, in Bradshaw's words, 'the most expeditious route from Scotland to Ireland.' However, Bradshaw mentions that Stranraer 'itself has no particular attraction.'

*Left:* Cumnock was a mining town, and Stepend bing dominated the town. Close by is Auchinleck, home of James Boswell, the famous author.

*Bottom left:* The ironworks of Muirkirk. Close to the ironworks was a golf course. Mineral railways crisscrossed the area serving the ironworks, the various local coal mines and Muirkirk itself.

the witches dancing to the sound of their master's bagpipe. Innumerable pilgrims from all lands visit these scenes, and the place of the poet's residence, to gaze on what has been charmed and sanctified by his genius, or merely to have the satisfaction of standing beneath the roof where Burns first saw the light.

## NEW CUMNOCK
Telegraph station at Auchinleck, 7 ½ miles.
   HOTEL – Crown.
   MARKET DAY – Saturday.
   BANKERS – Bank of Scotland.
Close by is Afton Bridgend Castle. Coal, with graphite and lead, abound in this neighbourhood.

## OLD CUMNOCK
   POPULATION, about 2,395.
   Distance from station, 2 miles.
   Telegraph station at Auchinleck, 2 miles.
   HOTEL – Black Bull.
   MARKET DAY – Saturday.
   FAIRS – Weekly in Jan. Feb and Dec., Thursday after 6th March, Wednesday after 6th June, 13th July, and 27th Oct.
   Here is Terrenzean Castle, a fine ruin. At Borland, the pretty seat of the Hamiltons, are the ruins of a chapel. Plane-tree snuff-boxes are made here.

## AUCHINLECK
   A telegraph station.
   HOTEL – Dumfries Arms.
   MARKET DAY – Saturday.
   FAIRS – Last Tuesday in August (for lambs).
   MONEY ORDER OFFICE at Old Cumnock.
   Here are remains of the Boswell's old castle, Dr. Johnson lived here in 1773, and the pious M'Gavin was a native. Close at hand are the ruins of Kyle Castle.

## MUIRKIRK BRANCH
LUGAR station.

## MUIRKIRK
   Telegraph station at Auchinleck, 10 ¼ miles.
   HOTEL– Black Bull.
   MARKET DAY – Saturday.

*Above and left:* Robert Burns lived in Mauchline in this little unassuming property. Close by was Poosie Nansie's Inn.

*Below:* Barr Castle, Galston, is a tower house but has since 1894 been used as a Masonic lodge. It is the oldest building used regularly as a Masonic temple.

At Prieshill is a memorial to John Brown, whom Claverhouse shot at his own door.

## MAUCHLINE

Distance from station, ¾ mile.
A telegraph station.
HOTEL –Black Bull.
MARKET DAY – Saturday.
FAIRS – Second and last Thursday in April, Wednesday after 18th May, 4th Wednesday in June, 1st Wednesday in August, Sept. 26th, Thursday after 4th Nov., and 4th Wednesday in Dec.

On Mauchline Moor is a church lately rebuilt, where Wishart preached in 1544; and here the royalists were defeated in 1647. At the Green is a stone on which is recorded the death of five persons by 'Bloody Dumbarton, Douglas, Dundee,' &c., in 1685. Burns wrote his 'Mauchline Belles,' &c., at J. Dow's and Poosie Nansie's Inns. Near at hand is Barskimming Bridge, erected by Sir T. Miller, of Glenlee, Gavin Hamilton's House, the Lugar, and Ballochmyle.

HURLFORD station.

## NEWMILNS BRANCH
## GALSTON.

POPULATION, about 2,538.
Distance from station, 2 ½ miles.
Telegraph station at Hurlford, 3 ½ miles.
HOTEL – Loudon Arms.
MARKET DAY – Saturday.
MONEY ORDER OFFICE.
BANKERS – Union Bank of Scotland.

Close at hand is Loudon Castle, seat of the Marquis of Hastings, Burr Castle, at which are many cairns, and an elm 24 feet in girth, and Wallace Hill, the retreat of that gallant hero, and where he defeated Fenwick.

## NEWMILNS

POPULATION, about 2,211.
Telegraph station at Hurlford, 5 ½ miles.
HOTEL – Black Bull.
MARKET DAY – Saturday
FAIRS –1st Thursday in February, 3rd Wednesday in May, 4th Thursday in August, Wednesday after 1st Tuesday in September, 4th Wednesday in October.

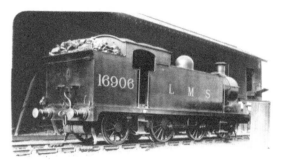

*Above:* Kilmarnock Cross, *c.* 1895.

*Left:* At Hurlford shed in LMS days is Glasgow & South Western Railway tank No. 16906.

*Below:* Not seen in Bradshaw's time was the tram. This is Kilmarnock's first electric tram.

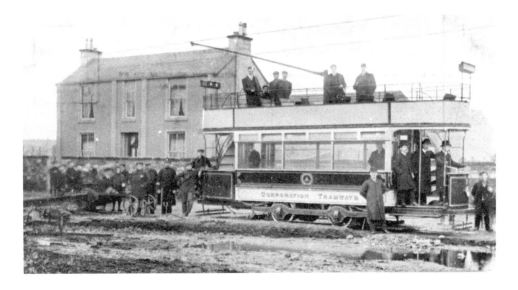

MONEY ORDER OFFICE at Mauchline, 2 miles.

In Ramsay's song the scenery near Paties' Mill, on the river, is described.

## KILMARNOCK
POPULATION, about 21,443.

A telegraph station.

HOTELS – George, Black Bull.

MARKET DAYS – Tuesday and Friday.

FAIRS – 2nd Tuesday in May, last Thursdays in July and October.

BANKERS – Branch of Bank of Scotland; Branch of Commercial Bank of Scotland; Branch of Union Bank of Scotland; Branch of Western Bank of Scotland.

In the vicinity are the Castle, and Baturre's Castle (in ruins), Catter Hill, at which a court is held, and black mail was levied here in 1744, St Marnoch, and Ardoch, the seat of W. Bontine, Esq.

## STEWARTON
POPULATION, about 3,164.

Distance from station, 4 ¼ miles.

Telegraph station at Kilmarnock, 4 ¼ miles.

HOTEL – Railway.

Considerable manufactures of woollen tartans, caps, Scotch bonnets, carpets, muslin, damask, &c., are carried on here. Corsehill, seat of Sir John Cunninghame, Bart., is close at hand.

## DALRY
POPULATION, about 2,706.

A telegraph station.

HOTEL – Black Bull.

Here the Scottish people rebelled against episcopacy. The church is situated on a hill, which is almost an island. In the vicinity are Auchinskeith, with its cave, and the Temple lands, which belonged to the Knights Templars, with several cairns.

## [ARDROSSAN, TROON, AND AYR BRANCHES]
## KILWINNING JUNCTION
POPULATION, about 3,265.

A telegraph station.

HOTEL – Eglinton Arms.

MARKET DAY – Saturday.

FAIRS – January 21st, and 1st Wednesday November.

Here are the ruins of a Franciscan Abbey, founded by Hugh de Morville,

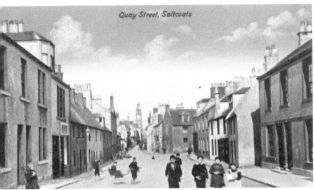

Quay Street, Saltcoats

*Clockwise from top left:* The SS *Viper* off Ardrossan. Ardrossan harbour had been built at great expense and the town was a centre for shipbuilding.

A model of the sailing vessel *Caledonian Frigate* hanging from the ceiling of Ardrossan parish church.

The *Glen Sannox*, a Clyde pleasure steamer, entering Ardrossan harbour, *c.* 1925.

In Irvine 'a considerable coal and shipping trade is here carried on by a population of about 7,534.'This view shows the town's harbour full of all types of ships.

Quay Street, Saltcoats.

in 1140. The church stands near the old spire of the abbey, the last abbot of which was Gavin Hamilton. An archery club is held here, which was established in 1488, and at which the popinjay is held.
STEVENSTON and SALTCOATS stations.

## ARDROSSAN
POPULATIONS, about 2,671.
A telegraph station.
HOTEL – Eglington Arms.
MARKET DAY – Saturday.
FAIRS – Tuesday before Ayr July fair, and 4th Thrusday in November.
BANKERS – Branch of Bank of Scotland.

A modern packet station and bathing place, in Ayrshire, on the Firth of Clyde, on a branch of the Glasgow & South Western, 5 miles from Irvine. This branch joins the main line at Kilwinning.

Steamers to Belfast. Sea passage, 6 ½ hours.

The fine mountain scenery of Arran and Bute fronts this beautiful port, which was founded a few years back by the Eglinton family, and has a fashionable reputation, with baths, terraces, crescents, hotels, &c. The harbour, on which two or three hundred pounds have been expended, lies within a point of land, giving name (Ard Ross, i.e., high head) to the parish, from which a circular pier runs out north-west towards the Horse Rock or island. Another rock, called Grinan, takes its designation from Grian, the sun, the worship of which appears to have been common with the Celts in pagan times. For instance, Grianan of Aileach, a celebrated sun-altar in Ireland.

Knockgeorgan hill, to the north-west of Ardrossan, is 700 feet high, and offers a striking prospect. Ardrossan Castle, now a ruin, was a seat of the Eglinton family, whose present residence here is the Pavilion.

## IRVINE
A telegraph station.
INNS –King's Arms, Wheat Sheaf.
MARKET DAYS – Monday and Saturday.
FAIRS – 1st Wednesday in January, 1st Tuesday in May, Wednesday before Ayr fair, 3rd Monday in August, and Wednesday after.

A considerable coal and shipping trade is here carried on by a population of about 7,534. Here is an old tower belonging to the Eglintons. Galt, and James Montgomery, the poet, were natives. Jack (who was called Mrs Buchan, who considered herself the woman of the 12th chapter of Revelations), held the living. Burns had a flax shop in Glasgow Vennel Street, which has been burnt down.

*Left:* Ayr Street, Troon. Troon was noted by Bradshaw for its rabbits and salmon.

*Below:* Three views of Ayr. The county town had a population of 17,624 and was an important port. The town itself, as well as being famous for Robert Burns, produced shoes, cotton goods, woollens, carpets and nails.

The town's importance was due to it being at the mouth of the River Ayr and its old and new bridges crossed the river close to the harbour. In 1315, Robert the Bruce, after his victory at Bannockburn the year before, held the very first Scottish Parliament at Ayr.

Cromwell based troops at Ayr and his men built walls around parts of the town.

The railways reached Ayr in 1840, although Kilmarnock had had its waggonway and subsequent railway for a good twenty years before this.

Burns Statue Square now dominates the centre of Ayr, as does the Glasgow & South Western Railway's Station Hotel.

## TROON

POPULATION, about 2,404.

Distance from station, 1 mile.

A telegraph station.

HOTELS – Portland, Commercial.

MARKET DAY – Saturday.

MONEY ORDER OFFICE.

BANKERS– Union Bank of Scotland.

Here is a pier 800 feet long, with revolving and fixed lights on it. Plenty of salmon and rabbits are in the vicinity.

MONKTON and PRESTWICK stations.

## AYR

A telegraph station.

HOTELS – King's Arms, The Ayr Arms, Commercial.

STEAMERS to and from Campbeltown, calling off Kildonan, Clauchog Shore, and South End of Arran, Girvan, and Stranraer, calling off Girvan and Ballintrae.

MARKET DAYS – Tuesday and Friday.

FAIRS – 1st Tuesday in January, last Tuesday in June, September 29th, and 3rd Tuesday in October.

BANKERS – Clydesdale Banking Company; the Royal Bank of Scotland; Union Bank of Scotland; City of Glasgow.

AYR, a port, parliamentary burgh (one member), and capital of Ayrshire, on the west coast of Scotland, at the mouth of the Ayr water, a picturesque stream, running between steep banks, from about 30 miles in the interior. Salmon and Water o' Ayr whetstones are produced by it. Population, about 17,624. About 5,000 tons of shipping are registered at the port, which has a pier harbour. Shoes, cotton and woollen goods, carpets, and nails, are the chief branches of manufacture.

Its old church of Cromwell's day, is on the site of a friary. About a quarter of a mile from St. John's Church is the Fort. At the latter place Bruce held a parliament to confirm the succession of the crown. Bruce's ancestors were Earls of Carrick. The southern is the most hilly of the three districts into which this county is divided, 'where Bruce ance rul'd the martial ranks, And shook his Carrick spear.' – Burns.

Ayr itself stands in the middle one, called Kyle, after Coyl or Coil, - 'Auld King Cole' of the old song.

There was an older church of the 13th century, of which a tower is left at the fort which Cromwell built in his Scottish campaign. It stood close to William the Lion's castle. The county buildings are copied from the Temple of Isis at Rome.

Burns' Cottage, Ayr, in 1862.

*Above:* Ayr's most famous son was born in Alloway and the above scene shows that his birthplace was a tourist attraction, even in 1862. Stovepipe hats were the fashion of the day.

*Left:* By 1896, the centenary of Burns' death, a display of photographs for sale hangs outside the entrance to Burns' cottage.

*Below:* Tourists gather at the grave of Robert Burns' parents, William and Agnes Burnes. The Burnes version of the name was used by Robert until 1766, when he began to use the familiar version of his name. Bradshaw was obviously well taken by the poetry of Robert Burns, quoting it extensively.

Close by is the new Gothic clock tower, 113 feet high, on the site of Wallace's tower (so called because the Scottish hero was imprisoned here); it supports a statue of Wallace, by Thom.

> We'll sing and Colla's plains and fells,
> Her moors red brown wi' heather bells,
> Her banks and braes, her dens and dells,
> Where glorious Wallace
> Aft bore the gree, as story tells,
> Frao Southron billes.

> At Wallace's name, what Scottish blood,
> But boils up in a spring-tide flood!
> Oft have our fearless fathers strode
> By Wallace's side,
> Still pressing onward, red wat shod,
> Or glorious died. – Burns

Thus sings the Ayrshire Bard, whose name is identified with the town, and almost every part of his native county. The oldest of the 'twa brigs' is a high, narrow, solid structure, on four arches, built in 1485, by two sisters, near the 'Ducat Stream', a ford just above it. About 100 yards off is the new bridge, built by Adam, in 1788, which gave occasion to the Brigs of Ayr. In this humourous dialogue, the poet describes the river at the time of the floods. And from Glenbuck down to the Ratton quay, 'auld Ayr is just one lengthened tumbling sea.' Glenbuck is at its source.

He refers again to the 'bonnie banks of Ayr', in what was meant to be his farewell song when leaving for Jamaica, 'The gloomy night is gathering fast.' About 2 ¼ miles out of Ayr, on the Maybole road, is Burns' Cottage, 'the auld clay biggin', in which he was born, in 1750. Further on is 'Alloway's auld hanted Kirk,' where he and his father, William Bruness (this was how the family name was spelt), 'the saint, father, and husband' of his Cottar's Saturday Night, are buried. It is a mere ruin, without a roof or rafters, the wood of which has been converted into snuff boxes, &c.; but the churchyard, which was walled round by Burns' father, is crowded with graves of the poet's admirers, who choose this as their last resting place. Burns put a stone over his father's grave, but this has been gradually carried away, and is replaced by another. Here Tam O'Shanter saw the witches dance –

> A winnock-bunker in the east,
> There sat auld Nick in the shape o'beast.

This window seat remains, divided by a mullion. About a quarter of a mile north-west, is a solitary tree in the field –
> By the cairn,

Kirkoswald Kirkyard, where Tam o' Shanter and Souter Johnny were buried.

"WHAT ARE THE WILD WAVES SAYING?—*NEAREST PUB' 7 MILES.*

*Left:* 'On a picturesque height above the road, commanding a view of these interesting localities, is Burns' Monument'.

Alongside the monument at Alloway, next to the old bridge, are two statues, one of Souter Johnnie and the other of Tam O'Shanter. Souter Johnnie's real name was John Davidson and he was a shoemaker and lived in Kirkoswald. The kirkyard he is buried in is shown in the top picture.

Just to the north of Kirkoswald is Dunure, famous for its castle, and, at the time this postcard *(left)* was sent in 1908, for being dry, the nearest pubs being in either Ayr or Girvan.

Whare hunter faud the murder'd bairn;

And a little further, on a small branch of the Doon, –
        The ford,
        Where in the saw the chapman smoor'd.

Close to the Doon was a thorn (now gone) –

        Abune the well,
        Where Mungo's mither hang'd hersel'.

Then comes the 'key-stane o' the brig,' which Tam, on noble Maggie, made such strenuous efforts to cross, pursued by the hellish legion.

    This river is the subject of one of Burns' sweetest songs – 'Ye banks and braes o' bonnie Doon.' Close to the bridge, on a picturesque height above the road, commanding a view of these interesting localities, is Burns' Monument, a small circular dome, surmounted by a tripod and other ornaments, resting on nine open Corinthian pillars, and a spreading basement in which are deposited Burns' bust, by Park, his portrait, by Nasmyth, the Bible he gave to his Highland Mary, and other relics. The design was by Hamilton, and the first stone was laid by Sir A. Boswell (son of Dr. Johnson's biographer), in 1820, with an eloquent speech. In the grounds of this monument are the two celebrated statues of Tam O'Shanter and Souter Johnnie, by Thom, the self-taught sculptor. These immortal heroes of what Burns justly looked on as his 'standard performance in the poetic line,' were Douglas Graham, a farmer of Shanter, near Kirkoswald, and John Davidson, a shoemaker (souter), of the same place, where both are buried. The scene is fixed at Jean Kennedy's Inn. Burns wrote *Tam O'Shanter* for Grose (who first published it in his *Antiquities of Scotland*), in return for the Captain's sketch of Alloway church.

    On the coast in this neighbourhood, is Colwan, or Culzean Castle, the noble seat of the Marquis of Ailsa, and, about 3 ½ miles above Burns' monument, on the banks of the Doon, is Cassilis Castle, still more ancient, and a favourite haunt of the fairies, which suggested his Hallowe'en.

        Upon that night when fairies light
        On Cassilis Downans dance,
        Or for Colean the route is ta'en, &c.

To the west, are the wild ruins of Dunure Castle, the fine seat of the same (Kennedy) family. Along the shore to the south stands Culzean Castle; and further still stands Turnberry Castle. In a direct line Culzean Castle

ON THE ROAD TO                    Riddel, GIRVAN.

Waiting for the Boats, Girvan.

A common tour in both horse and carriage days and in the early days of motoring, as depicted in the above view of a charabanc, was the tour from Girvan to Ballantrae.

Pleasure boats made cruises from Girvan harbour *(left)*, while the largest ships in the world, such as the *Lusitania (below)*, would do their speed trials off the Clyde, having been built there.

SS "LUSITANIA"
passing the CRAIG

will be nine, and Turnberry Castle twelve miles south-west from Burns' monument, at the latter of which Scott, in his *Lord of the Isles*, makes Bruce land from Arran by mistaking a signal, when his country was overrun by the English.

About 10 miles south-west, out in the sea, opposite the mouth of the 'Girvan's fairy-haunted stream,' is Ailsa Craig, a huge basalt rock, 1,100 feet high, and two miles round.

> Duncan fleech'd and Duncan pray'd,
> Ha, ha, the wooing o't;
> Meg was deaf as Ailsa Craig,
> Ha, ha, the wooing o't.
> Duncan sigh'd, baith out and in,
> Grat his e'en baith bleart an' blin',
> Spak o' lowpin' ower a linn;
> Ha, ha the wooing o't.

Christopher North said, he would give all he had written for that line, 'Spak o' lowpin' ower a linn.'

About 6 miles east of Ayr, is Coylton Kirk, and Mill Mannock, a quiet spot on the banks of the Coyl, the scene of *The Soldier's Return*. He was in an inn, at Brownhill, when a poor worn-out soldier passed the window, and put this sweet song into his head. At Ochiltree, on the Lugar water, Cumnock Road, Willie Simpson, one of the poet's early friends, and a brother rhymer, was schoolmaster:–

> Auld Colla now may fidge fu'faln,
> She's gotten poets o' her ain,
> Chiels wha their chanters sinna hain,
> But tune their lays,
> Till echoes a' resound again
> Her well-sung praise

> The Illissus, Tiber, Thamos and Seine,
> Glide sweet in monie a tunefu' line,
> But Willie, not your fit to mine,
> And cock your creat;
> We'll gar our streams and burnies shire
> Up wi' the best.

In ascending the Ayr from the town, you pass Auchincruive, a seat of the Oswalds, then Stair Kirk and Barskimney Bridge, where was the house

*Above:* Burns' parents rented Lochlea farm, which was situated in a low-lying area north of Tarbolton and Mauchline. It became the family home in 1777.

*Left:* In Catrine was a cotton mill, one of the first in the country, which opened in 1787 and was powered by two large water wheels. In the 1820s, the original wooden wheels were replaced by iron ones, of 50 ft diameter. Twelve foot broad, the wheels each had 120 buckets that would fill with 11 cu.ft of water to power the wheel. At 3 rpm, they used 210 tons of water per minute. From their inception, they were a tourist attraction and only finally ceased work in the 1940s.

of old Kemp, and the Mill which suggested his 'Man was made to mourn.' 'Catrine Lea,' Dugald Stewart's seat, near the Braes of Ballochmyle, where he first met young Lord Daer, and Sorn Castle, are higher up. South of this is Auchinleck House, the Boswells' seat, with Reynolds' portrait of Johnson's biographer. The Doctor was here in 1773.

> But could I like Montgomerie fight,
> Or gab like Boswell,
> There's some sark neck I wad draw tight,
> And tie some hose well.

Boswell, as might be expected, as fond of shining at public meetings.

A little north of Barskimmey is Mossgiel Farm, in Mauchline (or Macklin) parish. His humble farm house remains, with only one window in it. Here, when ploughing in 1785, the little field mouse led him to write his beautiful lines to the 'Wee, sleekit, cowrin' tim'rous beastie.'

> I doubt na whyles, but thou may thieve;
> What then, poor beastie thou maun live!
> A daimen icker in a thrave
> 'S a sma' request:
> I'll get a blessin' wi' the lave,
> And never miss't!

Here, too, his equally beautiful *Mountain Daisy*, 'Wee, modest crimson-tipped flower,' and his noble *Cotlar's Saturday Night* were written – the latter for his friend Aikin, a surgeon of Ayr. Another production of this period was his lines to James Smith, 'Dear Smith, the slee'est, paukiest theif.' It was in Smith's company that he dropped in one evening at Poosie Nansie's Inn, in the Cowgate, opposite the church, and witnessed something which suggested the Jolly Beggars. The churchyard was the scene of his *Holy Fair*; and W. Fisher, a Mauchline farmer, was the hero of *Holy Willie's Prayer*. Near the Church is Mauchline Castle, originally part of a cell to Melrose Abbey, the seat of another friend, Gavin Hamilton, the lawyer, and the poet's landlord. A new church has been built on the Moor; at the Green, is a stone, commemorating the death of five covenanters in 1615, by 'Bloody Dumbarton, Douglas, and Dundee.' At Morrison's, the carpenters' house, Burns wrote his spirited lines *To a Haggis* –

> Fair fa' your honest sonsie face,
> Great Chieftain o' the puddin' race!

A haggis is a pudding exclusively Scotch, but considered of French origin.

*From top to bottom:* The Masonic Lodge in Tarbolton, one of the earliest in the United Kingdom, was housed in this little thatched cottage. Robert Burns was a Mason and regularly visited this lodge only a few miles from Mauchline.

East Ayrshire was rich in mineral wealth and below the ground lay much coal and ironstone. Pits and collieries abounded in the district, as did iron works at Dunaskin and Murikirk. This view of Waterside, dated to about 1905, shows the mineral railway and the miners' rows of the small hamlet. The chimneys of the ironworks can be seen behind the row of coal wagons.

Burnside Street, Dalmellington, *c.* 1910. The railway to Dalmellington arrived in 1858 and the advent of steam engines to pump water from deep mines saw a rise in the area's coal industry.

The old Mill o' Beith. The town was known for its smugglers, some of whom did a daring raid on Irvine customs house in 1733 which saw much contraband spirited away. The famous Scottish poet Robert Tannahill had relatives who lived close by at Gateside, while Dr Henry Faulds, who developed the science of fingerprinting, was born in Beith some twenty years before this *Bradshaw's Guide* was published. The watermill shown here is located on the Roebank burn.

Its ingredients are oatmeal, suet, pepper, &c., and it is usually boiled in a sheep's stomach. Although a heavy, yet it is by no means a disagreeable dish.

Going back to Ayr from Mauchline, you pass Tarbolton, whose learned schoolmaster was the hero of Death and Dr. Hornbook, and the Mill on the river Faile.

> I was come round about the hill,
> And toddlin' down on Willie's Mill
> Setting my staff, &c.

Willie, was William Muir, of Tarbolton. 'Oh! Rough, rude, ready-witted Rankine' had a farm at Adam Hill. Another resident was Annie Ronald, the Annie of *Rigs o' Barley*.

Coilsfield, in this parish (so called because Coilus, the Pictish King was buried here) on the Faile, is the seat of the Montgomeries (Earls of Eglinton), at which Mary Campbell, his immortal 'Highland Mary', lived dairy woman; she was to have been married to Burns, but died in early life, and he never forgot her.

> Ye banks and braes and streams around
> The Castle o' Montgomerie,
> Green be your woods, and fair your flowers
> Your waters never drumlie!
>
> There simmerfirst unfauld her robes,
> And there the langest tarry;
> For there I took the last fareweel
> O' my sweet Highland Mary.

His exquisite lines to Mary in Heaven, 'Thou lingering star, with lessening ray,' were written at Mossgiel, on the anniversary of her death; and there can be no question that Mary was in his heart when he wrote his Ae' fond kiss, which Sir Walter Scott says contains the 'essence of a thousand love tales.'

### Ayr to Maybole and Dalmellington

By a further opening of the rails the tourist is enabled to continue his route to DALRYMPLE, CASSILLIS, and MAYBOLE to the right; and also to HOLLYBUSH, PATNA, WATERSIDE, and DALMELLINGTON to the left.

Glasgow and South Western Main Line continued

*Clockwise from top left:* The bandstand in Johnstone.

Paisley Road, Renfrew, with a tram heading for Paisley.

Renfrew had a ferry for many centuries and the steam ferry shown here dates from the early twentieth century. It travelled from Renfrew to Yoker, some 200 yards.

Shipbuilding yards could be found all along the river Clyde until the 1970s. Now only a couple remain on the river.

Looking down the Cart towards Paisley Abbey.

Abandoned and converted into a railway, this is one of the few remaining parts of the Paisley Canal today.

At BEITH is a Market on Friday, and Fairs 1st Friday in January, February, and November, and August 30th, and Witherspoon was minister in 1745.

LOCHWINNOCH, and MILLIKEN PARK stations.

## JOHNSTONE

POPULATION, about 5,872.
A telegraph station.
MARKET DAY – Saturday.
Near at hand are Johnstone Castle, seat of L. Honston, Esq., and Milliken, Sir W. Napier, Bart.

## PAISLEY

A telegraph station.
HOTEL – Saracen's Head.
FAIRS – Third Thursday in February and May, second Thursday in August and November; three days each.
RACES – Second Thursday in August.
BANKERS – Branch of British Linen Co.; Branch of Union Bank of Scotland; Branch of Bank of Scotland.

PAISLEY, is a thriving seat of the cotton trade, with a population of about 47,952, who return one member, and contains remains of a Norman priory, founded in 1164, by the ancestor of the Stuart line (who emigrated from Shropshire), large Town Hall, &c. On the castle site quarries of coal, stone, iron, &c., and alum work at Hurlet, and various old seats, as Stanley Castle, with its pillar cross, Carndonald, Cochrane, and Elderslie, which was Wallace's birth-place. The basalt rocks at the braes of Gleniffer are 760 feet high. Professor Wilson, the 'Christopher North' of Blackwood's Magazine, and Tannahill, the poet, were natives.

The ruins of the palace are worth a visit. In the vicinity are Hawkhead, Earl of Glasgow; Horsehill, T. Spiers, Esq.; Railston, J. Richardson, Esq.; Crookstone (where Queen Mary visited Darnley); Oakshare Head, and Stewart's Raiss.

## RENFREW

This county, which returns one member, contains many manufacturing towns and villages. It is bounded by the Firth of Clyde and Clyde River. The waters of this county are of no great magnitude in themselves; but by the industry and enterprise of the inhabitants of the adjacent district, they are rendered of considerable importance to society, by being made

*Clockwise from top left:* Fore Street, Port Glasgow, with timber filling the basin.

The James Watt Technical College was built on the site of Watt's birthplace.

In Bradshaw's time the sailing ship, here in Albert Dock, would have been a common sight

Greenock Princes Pier.

instruments of human industry, and made to toll for man. If they descend suddenly from a height, it is not from a picturesque cataract, or to please the eye or ear with the wild and beautiful scenery which nature delights to exhibit, but to turn some vast water-wheel, which gives motion to extensive machinery in immense buildings, where hundreds of human beings are actively engaged towards Glasgow, the great theatre and centre of Scottish manufactures and commerce, everything assumes an aspect of activity, enterprise, arts, and industry.

## GLASGOW, PAISLEY, AND GREENOCK

HOUSTON – In the church here are effigies of the Houston family: the ruins of the castle were used to build the village in 1780, in which is a pillar cross, 11 feet high. Close at hand are cairns, British kistvaens, and urns. A fair is held here on the second Tuesday in May.

BISHOPTON – The railway here runs through two tunnels of whinstone.

LANG BANK and PORT GLASGOW stations.

## GREENOCK

A telegraph station.

HOTEL – Tontine, George, White Hart.

STEAMERS to and from Glasgow, and all places on the Clyde, to Gareloch, Helensburgh, Roseneath, Garelochhead, Largs, Millport, Arran, Inverkip, Wemyss Bay, Strone, Kilmun, Kirn, Dunoon, Inellan, Rothesay, Ardrishaig, Crinan, Oban, Inverness, Fort William, Loch Fine, Loch Long, Arrochar, Lochgoilhead, Staffa, Iona, Ballachulish, Glencoe, Skye, Broadford, daily during the season.

MARKET DAY – Saturday.

BANKERS – Greenock Bank; Clydesdale Banking Co.; Branch Bank of Scotland; Branch of Royal Bank of Scotland.

GREENOCK, is a large seaport town on the southern bank of the Firth of Clyde (population about 36,680, who return one member), and the scenery in its vicinity is remarkable for its picturesque beauty. Greenock is indebted for its present commercial importance to the trade which was opened by the inhabitants of the West of Scotland with the American colonies after the Union. The new Custom House, created on a tongue of land which projects into the harbour, is one of the handsomest buildings in that part of Scotland. The principal street is nearly a mile in length, and there are others which run in a parallel direction along the quays, and are crossed by others at right angles; many modern improvements have recently taken place, which have greatly embellished the town. The harbour has been enlarged from time to time, and is now capable of admitting vessels of great burden. The manner in which this town is

*Top:* Greenock also had many shipyards. A cruiser being built for the Royal Navy.

*Left:* One of the many steamers essential for the Clyde Coast, the *Glen Sannox* being overhauled in Greenock, *c.* 1900.

*Below:* An 1890s image showing the PS *Galatea* and an unknown steamer, looking toward the Cloch, Gourock.

supplied with water, the aqueduct through which it is conveyed six or seven miles from the neighbouring hills to a reservoir over the town, are worthy of general admiration. Watt, the architect, was a native.

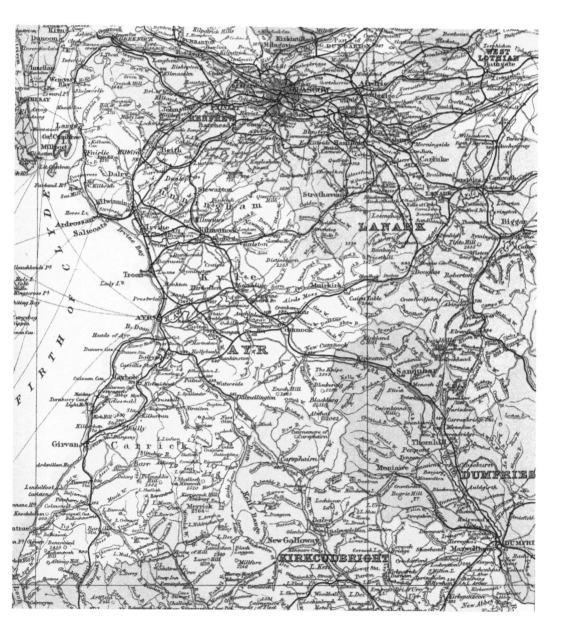

Carlisle, just over the border, was a busy railway centre where the lines of seven companies (three Scottish, four English) met. Having travelled north from Shap, the fall into Carlisle gave a rest before the steep inclines and summit at Beattock.

*Above and left:* Gretna Green was once the favoured choice of runaway grooms and brides. Above is Gretna from the station, and left is Carter's store in this little village, both *c.* 1910.

# Caledonian

Carlisle to Edinburgh and Glasgow.

## CARLISLE

The railway station in Court Square was built from a design by Mr. Tite, the architect of the London Royal Exchange, and of all the station houses on this line.

Upon starting from the station, the traveller will observe on his right hand the outer wall of the Castle, above that the front of the Deanery, and further over, the ancient towers of the Cathedral. On the left the canal to the Solway, and Dixon's factory. Proceeding onwards, we cross the Calder over a viaduct, and thence over the river Eden by another viaduct, after which the line proceeds through King Moor, and arrives at the ROCKCLIFFE, station. Leaving Rockcliffe, in a few minutes we arrive at the river Esk, which gives its name to Eskdale, one of the most beautiful places in Scotland. On the banks of the river, not visible, however, from the railway, is situated the 1st Sir James Graham's elegant mansion of Netherby.

Crossing the river on a seven-arched viaduct, we have a fine view to the north-west; thence passing over the Glasgow road, we can perceive the Solway on the right, and Langholm Hills, with Sir John Malcolm's monument on the left. We now proceed along the Guard's embankment, formed through a deep moss, which absorbed thousands of tons of earth before the foundation was sufficiently solid to bear a train. Shortly after this we reach the FLORISTON station. We then cross the Sark, and leaving the county of Cumberland, enter Dumfriesshire, one of the most important of the southern counties of Scotland.

The next station is now in view, and soon recognised as the celebrated

## GRETNA

Telegraph station at Carlisle, 9 miles.

HOTEL – Gretna Hall.

POST HORSES, FLYS, &c., at the station and hotel. Tariff – 1s 6d per mile; post boy, 3d per mile; one horse vehicle, 1s per mile or 15s per day; gig, 12s per day; riding horse, 6s to 7s per day; pony, 5s to 5s 6d per day.

MONEY ORDER OFFICE at Carlisle.

The village of Gretna Green, in Dumfries, Scotland, is built on the banks of the Solway Firth, eight miles north of Carlisle. It is the first stage in Scotland from England, and has for more than eighty years been known as the place for the celebration of the marriages of fugitive lovers from England. According to the

*Above:* Thomas Carlyle was still alive and writing when *Bradshaw's Guide* was published. His house in Ecclefechan is now a tourist attraction.

*Left:* 'Lochmaben is well worthy of a visit', not least for the statue of Robert the Bruce outside the town hall.

Scottish law, it was only necessary for a couple to declare before a justice of the peace that they were unmarried, and wished to be married, in order to render the ceremony lawful. An Act of Parliament has since come into operation which requires a residence in Scotland of too long a duration to suit the purpose of fugitive lovers, and the blacksmith of Gretna Green, like Othello, will now find his 'occupation gone'. More than 300 marriages took place annually in this and the neighbouring village of Springfield, and the fees varied from one to forty guineas.

Proceeding onward, the line passes the junction of the Dumfries line and Gretna Hall, through Graham's Hill cutting, and opens into a fine view, which about this point presents a most picturesque, varied, and highly romantic appearance.

Upon leaving KIRKPATRICK station the line soon crosses the 'gently winding Kirtle', on a viaduct of nine arches, and then passes the tower of Robert Gill, a noted freebooter, who, with many other reckless 'chields' of former times, made this district the scene of their border raids.

Shortly after leaving KIRTLE BRIDGE station we pass through an extensive cutting, and thence over an embankment. We then cross the Mein Water and West Gill Burn, and soon arrive at

## ECCLEFECHAN

Telegraph station at Lockerbie, 5 ½ miles.

HOTEL – Bush.

MARKET DAY – Saturday (large pork market).

FAIRS – Once a month.

The town of Ecclefechan is remarkable for nothing but its frequent and well-attended markets and fairs. From the station may be perceived a strong square keep or tower, the seat of General Matthew Sharpe, and known as Hoddam Castle, formerly a place of considerable importance as a border stronghold, and at present distinguished as one of the most delightful residences in Dumfriesshire. Opposite the castle, on a conspicuous mount, stands Trailtron, known as the Tower of Repentance, and formerly used as a beacon. It is said that Sir Richard Steele, while residing near this place, saw a shepherd boy reading his Bible, and asked him what he learned from it. 'The way to heaven', answered the boy. 'And can you show it to me?' said Sir Richard, in banter. 'You must go by that tower,' replied the shepherd, and he pointed to the Tower of Repentance.

Leaving Ecclefechan, we obtain a grand and extensive view of the surrounding scenery, perhaps the most gorgeous on the whole line. The Solway at the base of its gigantic sentinel; and beyond, the lofty Skiddaw, with its top melting away in the clouds. And before us is Borren's Hill, which from its curious shape is conspicuous long before we come near it. Skirting Brakenhill, we next arrive at the Milk Water, another of the poetical streams of bonnie Scotland, crossed by a viaduct, which commands a prospect of surpassing beauty.

*Left:* The last stone of a 'Druid's Temple' at Lochmaben. The stone itself is 118 cu. ft and weighs some 20 tons in weight. Scotland abounds with standing stones, crannogs, brochs and other archaeological sites.

*Below:* These two images of Beattock show the difference in steam engine technology in fifty years. Above is the now-preserved *Princess Elizabeth* of the LMS Princess-class of 1933 in British Railways livery. The lower image is a Caledonian Railway 4-4-0 locomotive of the 1880s.

LOCKERBIE

A telegraph station.

HOTEL – George.

MARKET DAY – Thursday.

FAIRS – Second Thursday in January, February, March, April, May, June, August, September, October, November, and before Christmas and Old Martinmas.

BANKERS – Branch of Edinburgh & Glasgow Bank.

Lockmaben, in the vicinity, is well worthy of a visit. It is poetically called the 'Queen of the Lochs', from its situation amid so many sheets of water. Looking north from this station, there being no curve, we can see down the line a very long way. Here 'Old Mortality' died at Brick Hall, in 1801. Lockerbie Hall, J. Douglas, Esq., and Mains Tower, which belonged to the Johnstones, are close at hand.

From NETHERCLEUGH station to the next there is scarcely an object of interest worth noticing. We pass Dinwoodie, Greens, and Mains, and then arrive at WAMPHRAY. Behind Raehill, a fine mansion situated on the banks of the Kinnel, towers the hill of Queensberry, one of the highest mountains in the south of Scotland. Shortly after leaving the Wamphray station, we cross the Annan, on a structure 350 feet in length. Farther on, a long embankment, succeeded by the Logrie cutting. Advancing, we cross once more the Glasgow road, and in a few minutes reach the place where all the visitors to Moffat will alight, at

BEATTOCK (Moffat)

A telegraph station.

HOTEL – Beattock.

MARKET DAY – Saturday.

FAIRS – Third Friday in March, July 29th, Oct. 15th and 20th.

MONEY ORDER OFFICE.

BANKERS – Branch of Union Bank of Scotland.

About two miles from Beattock, surrounded on every side but one by lofty hills, lies the fashionable village of

MOFFAT, celebrated for its mineral waters. The environs are remarkably beautiful, and the different villas exceedingly pretty. Moffat has long been farmed for its mineral waters (the sulphur Spa discovered in 1639, and the iron springs at Hartfell, in 1780), and visitors will find every accommodation, including Assembly Rooms, Baths, &c. Among the fine scenery scattered round Moffat, are Bell Craig, and the Grey Mare's Tall waterfall, the latter being one of the grandest sights it is possible to conceive. The water is precipitated over a rock three hundred feet high. In the vicinity are Raehills, Earl Hopetoun; Drumcrieff, formerly Dr Currie's seat. The Mole Hill, with its camps, and Bell Craig, which commands an extensive view, and where delicious whey milk can be procured.

Resuming our progress from the Beattock station, we proceed onwards through the lovely vale of Annandale, and then passing a deep cutting, we skirt

*Above, left:* A West Coast Route brochure from *c.* 1910. The railway lines which operated the routes to Scotland marketed themselves from an early age as East Coast and West Coast routes.

*Above, right:* Heather Jock, an Abington worthy.

*Below:* Elvanfoot was the junction for the Leadhills & Wanlockhead Light Railway, which took the passenger to the highest villages in Scotland.

the Greskin Hills, close to which are the sources of three of Scotland's finest rivers; the Tweed, the Clyde, and the Annan having their rise in the same clump of hills, and each falling into a different sea, in a different part of the kingdom.

The great viaduct over the Elvan is well worth attention. Passing ELVANFOOT station, where the Clyde and Elvan Water join, we reach

## ABINGTON

A telegraph station at Symington, 9 miles.

HOTEL – Hunter's

MONEY ORDER OFFICE at Biggar, 14 miles.

We now begin to perceive a distinct stream of the Clyde, which shortly after issuing from its source, from the accession of many tributary burns, becomes at this point, a river of considerable size, and keeps gradually increasing –

> Now sunk in shades, now bright in open day,
> Bright Clyde, in simple beauty, wends his way.

This is the junction of the Clyde and Glengowner water. Some gold was found here in the time of James VI.

Previous to arriving at the next station, we pass, on the right hand, Lamington Old Tower, one of the seats of the family, one of whose daughters, it is said, was married to the great Hero of Scotland, Sir William Wallace.

Passing LAMINGTON STATION, close to which are hilly sheep walks, porphyry, and good trout fishing, Lamington House, Wandell Bower, Windgate House, Arbery Hill (600 feet high), Whitchill (70 yards), Hartside, Woodend, and Braehead, with their Roman and Saxon camps, Druid arches, and Cauldchapel, with its moat of 20 yards, we arrive at

## SYMINGTON

A telegraph station.

A short time previous to reaching the station, we have the famous hill of Tinto appearing in view; towering high above the other giants of nature which surround it. Visitors ascend to the top of Tinto or the 'Hill of Fire,' in order to enjoy the fine view from its summit.

In the vicinity are Fatlips Castle, in ruins, and Castle Hill, which is plated all over.

## SYMINGTON, BIGGAR, AND BROUGHTON

This is a line, 19 ½ miles long, running out of the Caledonian, at Symington, to Peebles, 8 ¼ miles of which only are yet open. The line passes, via the station of COULTER to BIGGAR – A small town situated in a hilly district, with a population of about 1,550. The church, built by the Flemings, is in the form of a cross. Traces of a Roman camp may also be seen.

*Clockwise from top left:* Carstairs station was the junction for the line to Edinburgh.

The village itself was populated by people who worked on the railway.

Midcalder was a mile distant from the station that served the town.

Auchengrey Junction signal box.

Carnwath village.

BROUGHTON, in the vicinity of which are some border castle ruins. This forms the present terminus of the line.

THANKERTON and the neighbouring village of Corington Mill are celebrated as having been a favourite haunt of the persecuted Covenanters, and there are many spots pointed out among the surrounding hills as their places of worship. The Clyde, in the vicinity, is remarkable for its many windings.

Leaving Thankerton, and once more crossing the river, we shortly reach the Carstairs Junction, from which point the line forks; the right branch turning off to Edinburgh and the left to Glasgow.

CARSTAIRS JUNCTION

POPULATION, about 1,066.

A telegraph station.

MONEY ORDER OFFICE, Lanark, 5 ¼ miles.

Here are remains of the Bishops of Glasgow's castle, castle dykes, Roman camp of upwards of five acres, and Carstairs House, which is the seat of R. Monteith, Esq.

CARNWATH – Here are remains of Couthalley Castle, Carnwath House, the beautiful seat of the Somervilles, and the church, which contains their effigies and tombs. Here is also the kennel of the Linlithgow hounds.

AUCHENGREY and HARBURN stations, close to which is Harburn House, the seat of J. Young, Esq.

MIDCALDER

POPULATION, about 1,474.

Distance from station, 1 mile.

Telegraph station at Carstairs, 7 ½ miles.

HOTEL – Lemon Tree.

BANKERS – Edinburgh and Glasgow Bank.

Close at hand is Calder House, seat of Lord Torpichen, in which is a fine portrait of Knox, who first administered the sacrament here after the Reformation. Greenbank was the native place of Archbishop Spottiswoode, the church historian.

CURRIE – The scene of Ramsay's *Gentle Shepherd*, and near which is Currie Hill, the seat of the Skenes, and close by the ruins of Lennox Tower, the residence of Queen Mary and Darnley; Buberton, the hunting seat of James VI., and for some time the abode of Charles X of France, after the events of 1830.

KINGSKNOWE and SLATEFORD stations, at the latter of which fairs are held on the Wednesday after the 26th August and the Friday before Kirriemuir fair.

NEW LANARK

The Lake Pavilion, Lanark.

*Above:* New Lanark was the site of David Dale's cotton mill, now a World Heritage Site.

*Left:* Lanark Loch.

*Below:* Another revolutionary form of transport came to Lanark in 1910, when a huge aviation meeting was held at the Racecourse.

J. A. DREXEL

AVIATION GROUND, LANARK. TINTO in distance.

Carstairs to Glasgow

Proceeding on to Glasgow the line passes Carstairs House, the seat of R. Monteith, Esq.

From Carstairs station we cross the river Mouse, which runs through some wild and romantic scenery, arriving at

CLEGHORN, the junction of the branch to Lanark. Here are the ruins of an old chapel and a Roman camp.

LANARK BRANCH

Proceeding onwards, a distance of 2 ¾ miles, the whole of the neighbouring grounds to Lanark are remarkable as having been the hiding place of Sir William Wallace.

> Each ruggen rock proclaims great Wallace' fame,
> Each cavern wild is honour'd with his name,
> Here in repose was stretched his mighty form,
> And there he sheltered from the night and storm

LANARK

Telegraph station at Carstairs, 5 ½ miles,

HOTEL – Clydesdale

MARKET DAYS – Tuesday and Saturday.

FAIRS – Last Tuesday in February, second Wednesday in April, last Wednesday in May and July, first Tuesday in July, first Wednesday in November, and last Tuesday in December.

BANKERS – Commercial Bank of Scotland; City of Glasgow; the Royal.

From this point travellers can visit the Falls of Clyde, and the romantic scenery in the neighbourhood. Independent of the more than magnificent grandeur of the various waterfalls themselves, the beauty of the country on every side of the river, and the picturesque succession of views which present themselves to the eye at every turn of the road, are a source of great attraction. A guide to the Falls may be obtained at any of the respectable inns in the town.

The ancient town of Lanark, capital of the county, which returns one member, has a population of about 5,395, and although not engaging in outward appearance, possesses many points of interest, and it remarkable as having been the scene of Wallace's first grand military exploit, in which he killed Hoslerig, the English sheriff, and drove his soldiers from the town. The burgh consists of a principal street, and a number of smaller ones branching off. The grammar school had General Roy and Judge Macqueen as scholars. The church, built in 1774, contains a figure of Wallace. In the vicinity are Castle Hill tower, Quair Castle, Cleghorn, with its Roman camp, 600 yards by 420; Lee House, seat of Sir

*Above*: Some 1,700 men, women and children were employed at New Lanark.

*Left:* Station Road, Carluke.

*Below, left:* Milton Lockhart, Carluke. This house is now in Japan, having been removed there stone by stone.

*Below, right:* A private loco of Wm Baird & Co. at Gartsherrie Works. The iron founders could operate their locos on the main lines.

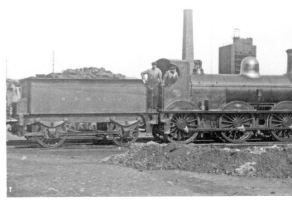

N. Lockhart, Bart., at which is the 'Lee Penny or Talisman.' Judge Lee, and Lithgow, the traveller, were born here.

NEW LANARK village is situated about one mile from Lanark, and contains a population of 1,807. It was established in 1784, by Robert Owen's father-in-law, the late David Dale, and is now the property of Messrs Walker & Co. There are several cotton mills, at which about 1,100 hands are employed. No stranger ought to omit visiting this far-famed village, which is quite in his way when visiting the Upper Falls of the Clyde.

THE FALLS – Bonnington Fall, athough the most inconsiderable, should be first visited, for the remarkable scenery surrounding it.

Curra Linn Fall, 84 feet, considered by some as the finest of the Falls, about half a mile from Bonnington, the seat of Sir Charles Ross, at which are Wallace's chair, cup, and portrait, is composed of three slight falls, at an inconsiderable distance from each other, over which the vast body of water rushes with fearful impetuosity into a deep abyss. To describe the beauties of the scene is an almost impossible task, requiring the glowing language of the poet to do justice to them.

Stonebyres. The approach to this (which is 70 feet) fall is by a gently winding road – its tout ensemble and the adjacent landscape is sublime. Above we have lofty crags fringed with natural wood. The torrent dashes in one uninterrupted stream into the abyss beneath, raising clouds of stormy spray from the boiling gulf.

Cartland Crags – which extends nearly half a mile on both sides of the river, is a most romantic dell, composed of lofty rocks, beautifully diversified with natural wood. The approach from the north – a level piece of ground, around which the Mouse makes a sweep – conducts to the mouth of this great chasm. As you enter, and through its whole extent, a succession of the most picturesque scenes appear on every hand. In the most sequestered part of the dell is a natural chasm in the rock, called Wallace's Cave, which tradition and history concur in informing us was often resorted to by that hero.

Upon emerging from Cartland Crags upon the south, the traveller finds himself surrounded by a beautiful amphitheatre of high grounds, open towards the Clyde, and in the immediate vicinity of the Bridge of Lanark.

Caledonian Main Line continued

Leaving CLEGHORN and BRAIDWOOD stations (near the latter of which are extensive collieries and lime works), we arrive at

CARLUKE

POPULATION, about 2,845.
Distance from station, ½ mile.
HOTEL – Commercial.
COACH to Lanark and the Falls of the Clyde.

The line now passes through a district of country rich in mineral wealth – beautiful scenery – celebrated far and near as the Orchard of Scotland, and famous for its fine fruit. The growers clear very large sums by sending the produce of their orchard to Glasgow. On the left side of the railway, shortly after leaving the station, is Milton, a handsome building, in the Tudor style of architecture, situated on a fine peninsula, and skirted on three sides by the Clyde. Next appears the stately seat of Mauldslee Castle, belonging to the Hyndfords, and St Oswold's chapel, a hermitage. The next station is

## OVERTOWN

Telegraph station at Motherwell, 4 miles.

All the scenery around is so enchanting that the traveller will wish the train to linger over it. Not far from this station is another beautiful spot called Cambusnethan, which attracts the notice and admiration of every stranger.

Passing WISHAW station, near which is Wishaw Castle, the seat of J. Hamilton, Esq. we reach

## MOTHERWELL

A telegraph station.

MONEY ORDER OFFICE at Wishaw, 2 ½ miles.

From this junction we pass the stations of HOLYTOWN and WHIFFLET to

COATBRIDGE – At this place the Dundyvan Iron Works are well worth visiting.

GARTSHERRIE JUNCTION – Proceeding a few miles beyond this station, we enter Stirlingshire.

## Caledonian Main Line continued

Pursuing our course from the Motherwell station, we pass several places of note. The beautiful village of UDDINGSTON is situated on an elevated spot, commanding an extensive and highly diversified prospect. The Clyde – the city of Glasgow, the Queen of the West – the numerous seats scattered around, the distant hills of Stirling, Dumbarton, and Argyllshires, lie extended before the eye, forming a panorama of great beauty. Then NEWTON station, and crossing the Clyde, we pass near

CAMBUSLANG – Loudon the naturalist was a native, and in the vicinity are Kirkburn, with the remains of a chapel and hospital; Westburne. T. Hamilton, Esq., and here 'Cambuslang Wark' took place in 1742, at which Whitfield was an eye witness. This station forms the junction of the

## STRATHAVEN BRANCH

The only intermediate station between Cambuslang and Hamilton is four miles from the junction, which requires a very short space of time to annihilate.

## BLANTYRE

In his visit, the stranger must not omit to see Blantyre Priory, Bothwell Bridge, where the Covenanters were defeated in 1679, by the Duke of Monmouth, and Chatelherault, a summer chateau of the Duke of Hamilton.

## HAMILTON

A telegraph station.

HOTELS – Commercial; Bruce's Arms.

MARKET DAY – Friday.

FAIRS – Last Tuesday in Jan., second Tuesday in Feb., Friday after 15th May, last Thursday in June, second Thursday in July and Nov.

BANKERS – Branch of Commercial Bank of Scotland; Branch of British Linen Co.

Over the whole neighbourhood of this place lie scattered scenes full of historical and poetical interest; and the traveller making it of his headquarters, might in a short time see a 'whole Switzerland of romantic dells and dingles.' Many of the places here are classic ground, the interest never flagging, from its being immortalised by the pen of Sir Walter Scott, and other writers of lesser note.

Hamilton Palace, partly as old as 1591, the seat of the Duke of Hamilton, is a noble building. The grounds and picture gallery, in which is Ruben's 'Daniel in the Lions' Den,' are thrown open to strangers, without any formal application. Cullen was a native of Hamilton. The traveller must of course visit the ruins of Bothwell Castle, one of the most picturesque and venerable monuments of the ancient splendour of Scotland. Its stately grandeur excites the admiration of all who have seen it.

From hence the railway passes the stations of HIGH BLANTYRE, MEIKLE EARNOCK, QUARTER ROAD, and GLASSFORD, to

Strathaven, supported principally by weaving and noted for the quality of its horses.

## Caledonian Main Line continued

We have scarcely got clear of the junction at Cambuslang than the arrival of the train is announced at the ancient royal burgh of

## RUTHERGLEN

Telegraph station at Glasgow, 2 ½ miles.

Here fairs are held on the first Friday after March 11th, 25th July, 25th August, May 4th, first Tuesday after June 4th, first Wednesday before first Friday in November, and first Friday after 25th December.

Rutherglen Church is famous on account of two great national transactions;

*Above, left:* Strathaven station in the 1950s.

*Above, right*: Hamilton Central Station.

*Left:* Stonefield, Blantyre

*Above, left:* Rutherglen on a fair day sometime about 1904. Traffic problems were just as bad then as today, albeit with different reasons for the congestion. This is likely to be St Luke's Fair, which was held in October each year.

*Above, right:* Rutherglen was the site of the 1297 treaty between England and Scotland that was supposed to bring peace between the two nations. The treaty was either signed in the kirkyard shown here, or in the church itself to the left. The tower dates from the fifteenth century, but the gable of the old church can clearly be seen. Rutherglen has been a place of worship since at least the sixth century.

it was here that Edward I signed the treaty in 1297, and Monteith covenanted to betray Wallace.

## GLASGOW

Telegraph stations at the Exchange, and 147, Queen Street.

HOTELS – Carrick's Royal Hotel; Walker's George Hotel; Bush's Buck's Head; McGregor's Queen Hotel.

RESTURATEURS – Ferguson and Forrester, 33, Buchanan Street; the Queen's, 81, Queen Street.

NEWS ROOMS – Royal Exchange, Queen Street, and the Tontine, (free); Athenaeum, Ingram Street, and the Telegraphic, 27, Glassford Street, one penny per visit.

COACH OFFICES – J. Walker, 104, West Nile Street; Wylie and Lochhead, 28, Argyle Street; A. Menzies, 10, Argyle Street.

STEAMERS to and from Ardrishaig, 5 ½ hours, Helensburgh, in 2 ½ hours,Roseneath, 2 ½ hours, Gareloch Head, 4 hours, Gourock and Ashton, 2 hours, Inverkip, 3 hours, Wemyss Bay, 3 ¼ hours, Largs, 3 ½ hours, Millport, 3 ¾ hours, Kilmun, 3 hours, Dunoon, 3 hours, Inellan, 3 ½ hours, Rothesay, 3 ½ hours, Strone 2 ¾ hours, Crinan, 7 ½ hours, Oban, 2 ¾ hours, Inverary, 7 ¼ hours, Arroquhar, 4 ½ hours, Lochgoilhead, 5 hours, &c.

MARKET DAY – Wednesday.

FAIRS – May 26, second Monday in July

BANKERS – Branch Bank of Scotland; Branch of British Linen Co.; Branch Commercial Bank of Scotland; Branch National Bank of Scotland; Branch Royal Bank of Scotland; City of Glasgow Bank; Union Bank of London; Clydesdale Banking Co.; Union Bank of Scotland; North British Bank; Branch of Edinburgh and Glasgow Bank.

GLASGOW – The first port and seat of manufacture in Scotland and a parliamentary burgh, two members, in the lower ward or division of Lanarkshire (which county also returns one member), on the Clyde, 50 miles from the open sea. That which was the ruin of many small places in this part of Great Britain, namely the Union, 1707, was the grand cause of the prosperity of Glasgow, which from its admirable position on a fine navigable river in the heart of a coal-field, and from the spirit of the inhabitants, has risen to be reckoned as the fourth port of the United Kingdom, and a rival to Manchester. When Bailie Nichol Jarvie and his worthy father, the deacon, 'praise to his memory,' lived in the Salt Market, before the American Revolution, it was a great place for the tobacco trade, but since 1792 cotton has been the staple business.

Population about 329,097, of which perhaps 50,000 are employed in the spinning, weaving, bleaching, and dyeing of cotton goods, worsted, muslin, silks, &c., while a large number are engaged in the manufacture of iron, brass, steam engines, glass, nails, pottery, umbrellas, hats, chemicals, and other branches of trade,

*Above:* A Caledonian Railway 4-6-0 leaves Central Station.

*Left:* Locomotives under construction in Hyde Park Works, Glasgow. From here they would be brought to the river and exported worldwide.

*Below:* Glasgow Bridge, *c.* 1895

and in wooden and iron ship building, besides numbers engaged in maritime and commercial transactions. These are the distinguishing characteristics of modern Glasgow, and the commercial activity and restlessness of its inhabitants have caused the immense impulse its trade has received within the last fifty years. The site is a level, four or five miles square, chiefly on the north side of the river. On the south side are the suburbs of Tradeston, Laurieston, and Hutchesonton; here are most of the factories. Its port is the open river, fronting the Broomielaw, lined by noble quays above one mile long, and so much deepened that first-class ships, which used to stop at Port Glasgow, 18 miles lower down, can now come up to the city. Formerly people could cross without wet feet, where now there is 20 feet of water. The tonnage owned by the port exceeds 150,000, its income is £90,000, and the customs (which in 1812 were only £3,100) amount to £700,000.

BRIDGES – Six cross the Clyde, in some parts 400 feet wide. Jamaica bridge, near the Ayr railway and Broomielaw, rebuilt by Telford in 1833, 500 feet long, 60 wide. A wooden bridge rebuilt in 1853, Victoria Bridge, rebuilt in 1851–3 by Walker, on five granite arches, the middle one being 80 feet span, and the next two 76 feet. It replaces old Stockwell Bridge, which was begun in 1345. Hutcheson Bridge built in 1833, by R. Stevenson, the builder of the wooden bridge, opened 1855. Rutherglen Bridge is the highest, near the King's Park, in which stands the Nelson pillar.

CITY AND COMMERCIAL BUILDINGS – The large new County Buildings are in Wilson-street. Justiciary or Law Courts, in the Salt Market, near Hutcheson Bridge, has a Grecian portico, imitated from the Parthenon. County Bridewell, Duke Street, an excellent self-supporting institution, built in 1824, in the Norman style. Large City Hall, in the Candleriggs-street, built in 1840. Old Town Hall in the Trongate – in front is Flaxman's statue of William IV. Exchange in Queen Street, a handsome Grecian building by D. Hamilton, erected in 1840, 200ft long by 76 broad; fine Corinthian eight-column portico and tower; news-room, 130 feet long. In front is Baron Marchetti's bronze statue of Wellington. Hamilton is also the architect of the Theatre Royal, in Dunlop street, and the City of Glasgow bank, the latter copied from the temple of Jupiter Stater. Union Bank and the handsome Assembly Room, now the Athenaeum, in Ingram street. Corn Exchange, in the Italian style, built in 1842. Trades' Hall, a domed building. Western Club House, in Buchanan street. Cleland Testimonial, in Sauchihall street, raised to commemorate the services of Dr Cleland to the city. Post Office, in George Square. Campell's warehouse in Candleriggs and Ingram streets. The Vulcan Foundry, belonging to Mr Napier, who established the steamers between this, Greenock, and Belfast in 1818, where iron steam-ships and engines for the great mail steamers are built. St Rollox's Chemical Works, north of the town, having an enormous chimney 440 feet high. Monteith's large cotton and bandana factory at Barrowfield.

CHURCHES – There are above 120 churches and chapels, the most conspicuous of which is St Mungo's High Church, on a hill at the top of High-Street. It was part of a monastery planted here by St Mungo (or Kentigern) in

From top left: Glasgow Bridge, being at the end of Jamaica Street, is also known as Jamaica Bridge. For a long time, the SV *Carrick* was berthed as a club for the Royal Naval Volunteer Reserve in Glasgow. Originally the clipper *City of Adelaide*, she sank at her moorings and was salvaged and 'parked' at Irvine, where she deteriorated and was so nearly scrapped. In 2014, she set sail for Australia and a full resoration, exactly 150 years after she entered service.

The Broomielaw, where steamers left for the Clyde Coast and Western Isles, with three pleasure steamers full of holidaymaker. The ships are the *Eagle III*, *Isle of Bute* and the *Benmore*.

Glasgow Necropolis in 1905. The graveyard had opened in 1833, soon after the Cemeteries Act had been passed, and contains the final resting places for many of the great and the good of the Second City of the Empire. Alexander 'Greek' Thomson designed numerous of the tombs as did Charles Rennie Mackintosh. The Blackie publishing family tomb was designed by Talwin Morris.

the 6th century, when the town was first founded, and was an Archbishop's Cathedral till episcopacy was abolished by the General Assembly which met here in 1638, in the Mace Church. It is a venerable stone building without transepts, 300 feet long, having a tower 224 feet high, and an ancient crypt of the 12th century, full of monuments, and once used as a church (see Rob Roy). There are about 150 pillars and as many windows. Close to it is the Barony Church. A short bridge crosses the ravine (here 250 feet deep) of Molendinar Burn to the Necropolis, where a monument to Knox was placed in 1845. St John's Church was Dr Chalmers's, many of whose labours and writings were commenced here. The College Church is as old as 1699. Tron Church tower as old as 1484; St Andrew's has a good portico; St George's, a spire of 160 feet; St Enoch's was built by Hamilton. Near the Custom House is the Gothic Roman Catholic Chapel. In George's Square are – Sir Walter Scott's monument, Chantrey's statue of Watt, the inventor of the modern steam engine, and Flaxman's of Sir J. Moore, the last of whom was born at Glasgow in 1761.

UNIVERSITY, SCHOOLS, &C – The University, in High Street, visited by Queen Victoria in 1849, one of the oldest buildings in the city, was founded in 1453, by Bishop Turnbull, and consists of two or three brick courts, in the French style, with a good staircase at the entrance; at some distance behind is Dr Hunter's Museum, in the Grecian style, containing objects of anatomy, natural history, books, autographs, illuminations, and Chantrey's bust of Watt, who was at first mathematical instrument maker to the University. The most curious thing is a Paisley shirt, woven without a seam or joining. The College Library includes about 80,000 volumes. The senior students, called togati, dress in scarlet gowns, and the whole number of 1,200 is divided into nations, according to the district they come from. Beyond the Museum is Macfarlan's Observatory.

Andersonian University, in the old Grammar School, George Street, is a place for gratuitous lectures, by the professors attached to it, among whom such names have appeared as Birkbeck, Ure, and Combe. It has a museum of models. The High School behind it was rebuilt in 1821. The Normal School, a handsome Tudor building, is near Garnet Hill, which commands a fine prospect. The Mechanics' Institution is in Hanover Street, near the Andersonian University. The Royal Infirmary, the Blind, and the Deaf and Dumb Asylums, are near the Cathedral, and the Town's Hospital and Magdalen Asylum are not far from these; the former, shaped like a St George's cross, with a dome in the centre. Hutcheson's Hospital or Asylum, with a spire, is in Ingram Street, near the Post Office; the new Lunatic Asylum, at the west end of the town, is in the Norman style.

The most bustling parts are in Buchanan Street, Argyle Street, the Broomielaw, &c.; and in the oldest quarters are Trongate, High Street, Stockwell Street, &c., round the cross; in Bridgegate stands the steeple of the old Merchant's Hall; Woodside and Elmbank are two of the finest crescents, not far from the Kelvin. The West End Park

*Above, left and right:* The contrast between Cathedral and back street slum is noteworthy. From the 1870s attempts were made to demolish the slum housing in the city and a fabulous record by Glasgow photographer Thomas Annan was taken of the shocking housing conditions mentioned opposite. *Below:* In contrast, one could sail from Glasgow to the most beautiful countryside in the world – the Western Highlands and Islands, via the ships of David MacBrayne.

is said to be one of the finest in Britain. At Port Dundas, the Forth and Clyde canal terminates; and at Bowling, some miles down the Clyde canal terminates; and at Bowling, some miles down the Clyde, near Dumbarton, is a Pillar to the memory of Henry Bell, who tried the first steamer on the Clyde, the 'Comet,' in the year 1812. Though the first cotton factory was Monteith's, in 1795, yet calicoes were woven here in 1742, and the check union kerchiefs of linen as early as 1700, at Flakefield.

## Glasgow to Iona

There is not within the limits of the United Kingdom a succession of more beautiful or varied scenery than in the route from Glasgow to Oban, Oban to Staffa and Iona, round the island of Mull. Glasgow is an admirable station for the tourist. It is within an easy distance, either by rail or steam-boat, of some of the most celebrated portions of the Western Highlands, and any traveller for pleasure, who finds himself within its smoky and dingy precincts, without having fully decided on the route he intends to take in search of the picturesque, beautiful, and romantic, has only to choose the first conveyance westward, whether it be a Greenock train, or a Clyde steam-boat, or Dumbarton coach, to find what he seeks, and to be gratified. Glasgow itself is supposed to offer few attractions to the tourist, but this is a mistake. Old Glasgow, with all its dirt and discomfort, the swarming wretchedness and filth of the celebrated 'Salt Market,' the 'Goose Dubs,' the 'Gallowgate,' and the 'Cowcaddens' is well worthy of a visit, if it were only to see how quaint, and even picturesque, in misery, are the haunts of the poor population of one of the richest cities in the world; consequently the traveller should not omit to take a glance at these places and the Wynds, which will be sufficient. Glasgow is in other respects an interesting place. Forty years ago, there were scores of towns within the limits of the kingdom which were superior to it in wealth, extent, and population. It has now no superior or equal except London. It has a larger population than Edinburgh, Dublin, Liverpool, or Manchester; and combines within itself the advantages possessed by the two last mentioned. Like Manchester, it is a city of tall chimnies and daily increasing manufactures; and like Liverpool, is a commercial port, trading extensively with every part of the known world. Its population amounts to nearly 330,000 souls, of whom 60,000 are Irish. Its prosperity is entirely owing to the industry, perseverance, and intelligence of its inhabitants. The new city of Glasgow, which is rapidly rising to the north-west of the ancient town, is one of the most splendid in Europe, and is not surpassed for beauty of architecture in its public and private buildings, the length, breadth and elegance of its streets, squares, and crescents, even by Edinburgh itself – renowned in all these respects though the latter may be. The motto upon the city arms is 'Let Glasgow flourish.' It has flourished, and bids fair to flourishing more.

There are several routes from Glasgow to Oban. One is by steam-boat from the Broomielaw, down the magnificent river Clyde as far as Bowling; from Bowling by railway to Balloch, at the foot of Loch Lomond; from Balloch by steam-boat on

*Above, left:* Glasgow's first railway was the Garnkirk & Glasgow, used to carry coal into the city from the Monklands. It is no coincidence that it terminated close to the Tennant's chemical works, with the tallest chimney in Britain, and access to both Monkland and Forth & Clyde Canals.

*Above, right:* The harbour at Bowling, on the Forth & Clyde Canal, was used to lay up paddle steamers over winter.

*Left:* A stunning brochure cover for the *Columba* and *Iona. Columba* was the longest Clyde steamer and lasted from 1879 until 1935, when she was scrapped.

this renowned lake, up the river Falloch to Inverarnan, at the other extremity; and from Inverarnan by coach to Inverary and Oban. The tourist by this route has the advantage of seeing Loch Awe, and its mighty lord paramount, Ben Cruachan, a loch and mountain not so much spoken of as Loch Lomond and Ben Lomond, but by no means inferior, and, in the estimation of many, far superior to them both. Another route to Oban is by steamer to Ardrishaig at the entrance of the Crinan Canal, through the Crinan in the track-boat to Loch Crinan; and from Loch Crinan in another steam-boat to Oban, the whole distance being performed in less than twelve hours. By this route the tourist passes through the pretty Kyles of Bute, and amid the magnificent coast scenery of the mainland of Scotland and the Island of Mull. The whole of this district is classic ground, and the reader of modern poetry will be reminded at every turn of the paddle-wheel of some incident recorded in poem, song, or drama, by Ossian, Sir Walter Scott, Wordsworth, Joanna Baillie, Thomas Campbell, and others.

The third route, which requires some pedestrianism, is equally attractive. From Glasgow to Greenock by rail, from Greenock to Kilmun, on the Holy Loch, by steam-boat; and from Kilmun along the side of Lock Eck to Strachur, a walk of 18 miles brings the traveller to the shores of Loch Fyne, where, if he does not relish another walk of 10 or 12 miles, round the head of the loch, he can take the ferry-boat, and be rowed 5 miles across to Inverary. From Inverary to Dalmally, and from Dalmally to Oban, which will afford the pedestrian two days' delight amid some of the most magnificent scenery in Scotland, indluding the river Achray and its beautiful falls, Kilchurn Castle, Loch Awe, Ben Cruachan, the Pass of Awe – worthy of its name; Connell Ferry, Loch Etive, and Dunolly and Dunstaffnage Castles, renowned in many a song and legend, and deserving all renown, not only from past history, but for the present grandeur of their ruins, and the splendour of their sites.

At Oban, during the summer season, a steamer plies regularly round the Island of Mull, calling at Staffa and Iona. Mull was pronounced by Dr Maculloch, in his 'Hebridean Travels,' a 'detestable island,' but other travellers have not participated in his dislike. On the contrary, Mull is pronounced by all who have sailed round it, or set a foot on it, to be a magnificent island; and though not possessing the advantage of good roads in the interior, and being in other respects in a very primitive state, it possesses manifold attractions for the sportsman, tourist, botanist, geologist, and the man who loves now and then to see human nature as it exists out of the beaten tracks of civilization. But as Iona and Staffa offer attractions of another kind, and enjoy a fame that extends wherever the English tongue is spoken, the great majority of tourists are in too great a hurry to visit them to spend much of their time in Mull. The island, moreover, is not rich in hotel accommodation, except at the one inn of Tobermory, the only town in the island.

Iona, or Icolmkill (the Island of Colm's Church), may be truly called an illustrious spot. It would take a volume to do justice to the claims which Iona has upon the attention of both the scholar and traveller.

*Left:* The steamer *Linnet* on the Crinan Canal in the 1880s.

*Below:* Crowded with holidaymakers, the paddle steamer *Edinburgh Castle* arrives at Carrick Castle.

## DUMBARTONSHIRE RAILWAY

Glasgow to Dumbarton, Helensburgh, and Loch Lomond.
Leaving Glasgow we reach the station of MARYHILL, the Junction of a line through BEARSDEN to the cotton bleaching village of MILNGAVIE. Soon after leaving Maryhill we enter

## DUMBARTONSHIRE

Anciently called the Shire of Lennox, and returning one member. The county consists of a mixture of natural pasture, wood, and arable lands. Five miles to the north-west of Dumbarton the traveller from the south obtains the first view of the celebrated Loch Lomond, the most beautiful and picturesque of all the Scottish Lakes. The circumstance which renders Loch Lomond more interesting than other great pieces of water, seems to be the woods in its vicinity; the variety of its romantic islands crowned with trees, and the vicinity of the gigantic Grampians, affording a striking contrast to the rich and placid scenery which is exhibited within the immediate neighbourhood. On an eminence to the southern extremity of the lake the whole beauties of this delightful expanse of water appear in full view. The prospect from the summit of Point Firkin, is also very fine, as it includes a view of the towering Ben Lomond, one of the loftiest of all the Grampians.

DALMUIR, and KILPATRICK stations.

## BOWLING

Telegraph station at Glasgow, 12 ¼ miles.
INN – Frisky Hall.
MONEY ORDER OFFICE at Dumbarton, 4 miles.
Here is a handsome revolving light.

## DUMBARTON

Telegraph station at Glasgow, 15 ¾ miles.
MARKET DAY – Tuesday
INNS – King's Arms, Elephant.
FAIRS – Third Tuesday in March and May. Thursday before Easter, first Wednesday in June, second Tuesday in August and November.
BANKERS – Branch of Commercial Bank of Scotland.

DUMBARTON, is built in a level tract of country, near the confluence of the river Leven with the Clyde. It consists principally of one handsome crescent formed street, with several smaller ones diverging from it. It has also the advantage of possessing a spacious and convenient harbour. It contains about 5,445 inhabitants, chiefly employed in the manufacture of glass, who return one member.

The ancient Castle of Dumbarton, the Dumbritton (Britons' Fort) of the Attacote, stands on the summit of a high and precipitous rock, and is a place of great strength and antiquity. From the top of the castle may be seen some of the finest and most extensive views in the whole of Scotland. From the batteries the visitor should ascend to Wallace's Seat, 560 feet high and a mile round. Here the patriot's sword is kept, and Queen Mary sailed from this place to France in 1548. A garrison is kept up here by the Act of Union. Colquhour, the author of 'Police of London' was a native, 1745. Looking towards the north is seen Loch Lomond, bounded by rugged mountains, among which Ben Lomond is conspicuous, rearing its pointed summit far above the rest. Between the Lake and Dumbarton is the rich vale of Loven, enlivened by the windings of the river. Turing eastward the Clyde is seen forming some fine sweeps. Douglas Castle appears on the left. Beyond the Clyde the distant country is very rich; and on a clear day the city of Glasgow may be discerned, particularly towards the evening. The prospect down the Clyde is no less interesting. The river expands into a large estuary, occupying a great part of the view; beyond are high mountains, whose rugged outlines and surfaces are softened by distance, or what painters call perspective; and under those mountains, on the left, are directly seen the town of Greenock and Port Glasgow.

*Clockwise from above:* One of the first marine steam engines made by Robert Napier was once located under Dumbarton Castle. The 1823 engine from the PS *Leven* is now in the maritime museum in Dumbarton.

Dumbarton High Street, *c.* 1900.

The brand new Cunarder *Aquitania* leaves the Clyde in May 1914.

The training ship *Empress* at Row in the Gareloch.

CARDROSS station.

## HELENSBURGH
Telegraph station at Glasgow, 24 miles.

This large and commodious watering place extends a considerable distance along the banks of the Clyde, at the mouth of the Gareloch, with Glenfuin extending behind. It was founded by Sir James Colquhoun, about 80 years ago, and is now become a place of growing importance.

## GARELOCHEAD
A small village, situate at the head of Gare Loch, and from whence there is a very beautiful drive along the side of Loch Long to Arrochar, a quiet though much frequented retreat during the summer months from its delightful situation on the margin of the loch and in the midst of mountain scenery. It is only two miles across the pass from this point to Tarbet on Loch Lomond. From Garelochead we retrace our journed to Dumbarton. We then pass the stations of DALREOCH, RENTON and ALEXANDRIA, and arrive at

## BALLOCH
Telegraph station at Glasgow, 20 ½ miles.

HOTEL – Railway

STEAMERS up and down Loch Lomond daily in summer, calling at Tarbet on Loch Lomond. From Garelochead we retrace our journey to Dumbarton. We then pass the stations of DALREOCH, RENTON and ALEXANDRIA, and arrive at

## BALLOCH
Telegraph station at Glasgow, 20 ½ miles.

HOTEL – Railway

STEAMERS up and down Loch Lomond daily in summer, calling at Tarbet and Inversnaid, the landing places for Inverary, Loch Katrine, and the Trossachs.

MONEY ORDER OFFICE at Alexandria, 3 miles.

Here are several mills, and an old castle of the Lennoxes.

## LOCH LOMOND
Telegraph station at Glasgow, 20 ¾ miles.

HOTELS – Ardlin Inn, at the northern extremity; Tarbet Inn, on the western shore, Rowardennan Inn, on the eastern shore.

MONEY ORDER OFFICE at Alexandria, 4 miles.

LOCH LOMOND is a large lake lying between Dumbarton and Stirlingshires, and may be said to belong to both, as the boundary line which separates the two counties passes through it. Loch Lomond is justly considered one of the finest lakes

*Clockwise from top left:* A piper at Tarbert, Loch Lomond, in 1935.

*Princess May,* a pleasure steamer on Loch Lomond.

Craigendoran pier with three North British Railway steamers. A railway station was located at the landward end of the pier.

Helensburgh goods shed in 1935.

in Scotland, and we cannot better describe it than in the words of Dr Maculloch: –

Loch Lomond is unquestionably the pride of our lakes; incomparable in its beauty as in its dimensions, exceeding all others in variety, as it does in extent and splendour, and uniting in itself every style of scenery which is found in the other lakes of the Highlands. I must even assign to it the palm above Loch Katrine, the only one which is most distinguished from it in character, - the only one to which it does not contain an exact, parallel in the style of its landscapes. As to the superiority of Loch Lomond to all other lakes, there can be no question. Everywhere it is, in some way, picturesque; and everywhere, it offers landscapes, not merely to the cursory spectator, but to the painter. From its richness of scenery it presents more pictures than all the lakes of the Highlands united. It possesses, moreover, a style of landscape to which Scotland produces no resemblance whatever. This is found in the varied and numerous islands that cover its noble expanse; forming the feature, which above all others, distinguishes Loch Lomond, and which, even had it no other attractions, would render it what it is in every respect – the paragon of Scottish lakes.

Boats can be hired at Balloch, for visiting the islands and points of interest on the Loch. A steamer is provided for places more remote. The following are a few places of interest, and should not be left unnoticed: – Lennox Castle, Inch Cailliach, near Bealmahn Pass, Banachra Castle, opposite Glen Fruin, where the Macgregors beat the Colquhouns (sounded 'Cohoon') of Luss, and Rowardennan, where the ascent of Ben Lomond is made – a mountain, 3,240 feet above the sea. At Inversnaid there are ponies ready (make a bargain beforehand), to take you to Loch Katrine, 5 miles, passing through Rob Roy's country. Ben Venue, 2,800 feet, is on the south side of Loch Katrine, which is surrounded by the scenery of the 'Lady of the Lake.' Then the wild Trossachs Pass, under Ben An, a mile long, to Loch Achray inn; the bridge or 'brig' o' Turk, Loch Vennachar, and Callander, at the foot of the Highlands; and down the Teith to Stirling, about 35 miles from Loch Lomond.

From Glen Falloch, at the top of Loch Lomond, you may go to Killin and Loch Tay, in Breadalbane; or to Tyndrum, Glencoe (a wild spot), and Fort William, for Inverness or Glenorchy (under Ben Cruachan); Benaw, and Oban (where the steamer stops), for Inverness, or Isle of Mull; or to Arroquhar and Inverary Castle, the Duke of Argyll's seat on Loch Fine, and Kilchurch, on Loch Awe.

## GLASGOW AND CROFTHEAD

This is a line 8 ¾ miles long. With the exception of Sir J. Maxwell's seat at POLLOCKSHAWS, rebuilt in 1753, where are some old state papers, and amongst them 'a Solemn League'; and Upper Polloch (the residence of Sir R. C. Pollock, Bart.), the line presents no particular feature of importance.

KINNISHEAD and NITSHILL stations.

BARRHEAD and CROFTHEAD are occupied principally by cotton spinners.

## GLASGOW AND AIRDRIE

From Glasgow, we pass the stations of STEP'S ROAD, and GARNKIRK, near which is the fine seat of J. Dunlop, Esq.

## GARTCOSH station

GARTSHERRIE has very extensive coal and iron works.

## AIRDRIE

Telegraph station at Coatbridge.

HOTEL – Royal.

MARKET DAY – Thursday.

FAIRS – Last Tuesday in May, and third Tuesday in November.

BANKERS – Bank of Scotland.

This town is situated in the centre of the Scottish coal district, which has caused its present prosperity. It was the ancient Arderyth, where in 577 Rydderech defeated Aidan. Bathgate may be reached from this place by rail, 19 ¾ miles distant. At Monkland Well is a good mineral spa, and Airdrie House is the seat of Miss Mitchelson.

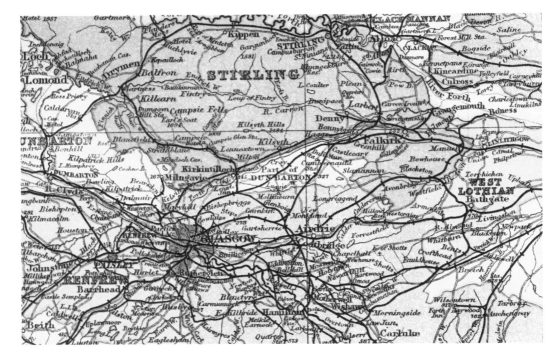

# Scottish Central

Which returns one member, and occupies the centre of the country between the Firths of Forth and Clyde, and, therefore, descends towards each of these streams, being highest in proportion to its distance from each. The principal mountain in this county is Ben Lomond, the view from which is grand and interesting beyond conception, and must be seen to be appreciated. At the bottom is seen the beautiful Loch Lomond, stretched out like a mirror; its islands having lost their rugged forms, and appearing as level surfaces, amid the bright expanse. The banks of the lake are seen ornamented with villas and cultivated grounds. Towards the east, the rich plains of Lothian and Stirlingshire are distinctly spread out to the sight. From thence to the south, and pursuing the view towards the west, the high grounds of Lanarkshire, the vales of Renfrewshire, with the Firth of Clyde, with its islands, and the wide Atlantic, are clearly discerned; while the Isle of Man, and the coast of Ireland, blended as it were with the sky, are scarcely discernible. But to one unaccustomed to Highland scenery, the most striking view is undoubtedly on the north side, which may in truth be termed fearfully sublime. The eye, from where it first discovers the Ochil hills, near the east, ranging along the north till it comes near the western ocean, beholds nothing but mountains, elevating their summits in almost every variety and forms, and which are covered with snow for a considerable portion of the year.

SCOTTISH CENTRAL

Greenhill to Stirling

GREENSHILL JUNCTION – Trains from Glasgow and the south unite here with this line, beyond which circumstance the station possesses no extraordinary attraction.

LARBERT

Telegraph station at Falkirk, 3 miles.

MARKET DAY – Saturday.

FAIR – Last Wednesday in April.

Close at hand are some ruins of Danish forts, and Larbert House, seat of J. Riddell, Esq.

To facilitate the traffic to and from Edinburgh and the north, a short branch line turns off here, running into the Edinburgh and Glasgow railway at Polmont.

At FALKIRK, a station midway between Larbert and Polmont, a line turns off to the left.

GRANGEMOUTH, a bonding town of importance, on the Firth of Forth, and telegraph station.

BANNOCKBURN

POPULATION, about 2,000.

*Clockwise from top left:* Larbert main street. Larbert is close to the junction for the line to Falkirk Grahamston station and the first station on the Scottish Central Railway.

Beaton's Mill, Bannockburn, where James III was murdered.

The Station Hotel in Stirling, now demolished.

Stirling Castle from the Back Walk in the 1860s.

King Street, Stirling. The Golden Lion Hotel is located on the right hand side of the street. Further up King Street, a beautiful Arcade takes you down close to the railway station. Stirling station was designed by James Millar, who also created Turnberry Hotel and Glasgow Central station.

Telegraph station at Stirling, 2 ½ miles.

HOTEL – Bruce's Head.

The rivulet called 'Bannockburn' here runs through a glen, and after a few miles falls into the river Forth. The inhabitants are very industrious, and carry on a considerable trade in carpets, tartan, and woollen cloth in general. It was here that the celebrated battle was fought between Robert Bruce, King of Scotland, and Edward of England, on the 24th of June 1314. Here James III was defeated in 1488 by his own subjects. Upon the top of an eminence, called Caldon Hill, and close by the side of the road, is a large earth-fast mountain limestone stone, on which the Scottish King planted his standard at the above battle; and so highly is this stone valued by the Scottish people, that fragments of it are frequently cut off, and set in rings, brooches, &c., and worn as a memorial of one of the proudest days in the annals of Scotland. Randolph's Field, Ingram's Crook, and Gillie's Hill are close at hand.

## STIRLING

A telegraph station.

HOTELS – Golden Lion (late Gibbs); Royal.

MARKET DAY – Friday.

FAIRS – First Friday in February, last ditto in March, first ditto in April, last ditto in May, first ditto in August, third ditto in Sept. And Oct., first ditto in Nov., second ditto in December.

BANKERS – Branch of Bank of Scotland, Clydesdale; Royal; Branch of Commercial Bank of Scotland; Branch of Edinburgh and Glasgow Bank; Branch of Union Bank of Scotland; Branch of National Bank of Scotland; City of Glasgow.

STIRLING, a county and garrison town, is built on an eminence in the centre of a fertile plain, which is watered by the river Forth, and above the town rises the Castle of Stirling, so celebrated in Scottish history. The stream which flows by the town is here of considerable depth, and vessels are able to unload their goods on the excellent quay by which it is bordered.

This ancient seat of the Scottish kings, and capital of Stirlingshire, is situated on a beautiful part of the Forth, about half way between Edinburgh and Perth. One member is returned for Stirling and its sister burghs. Population about 12,837. As a key to the Highlands it is an important position, having been frequently contested, and at length became the favourite seat of all the James's, from James I to James VI (or first of Great Britain). The best part of the Palace, or Castle, was begun by James V, the Knight of Snowdon, a hero of the *Lady of the Lake*, known also as the 'Gudeman of Ballangeich,' an alias conferred on him from his taste for disguises and intriguing adventures. The 'Gaberlunzie man,' and 'We'll gae nae mair a roving,' are founded on these. Ballangeich is the pass leading to the rock (350 feet high) on which the castle is perched, originally called Snowdon, and overlooking the town – one of the most splendid prospects in Scotland, especially of the Forth and Teith, and the distant Highlands. The oldest portion of the castle is the closest in which James II stabbed William Earl Douglas. The Parliament Room (120 feet long), with an oak roof, was built by James III, but is now a barrack, as also is the presence chamber in James V's palace – this fortress being one of the four which the Articles of Union, in 1762, provides shall be maintained. James VI added a chapel, which is now the armoury. He was educated here, under the care of the learned Buchanan. The ancient walls, drawbridge, &c., remain. In the park behind is a ring for tournaments. To the north-east of the Castle is the Moat Hill, commonly named Hurley-Hacket; on it executions generally took place. The old portion of the Castle was destroyed by fire 1855. The building is in course of re-erection, strictly in keeping with its former quaint style. The pulpit of the great reformer, Knox, is shown in the armoury, alnong with many other relics of the olden time. Argyll's Lodgings, in Castle Wynd, is now the military infirmary. Here the Duke of York and his daughter (afterwards Queen Anne) lodged in 1681.

The Grey Friars' Church was erected in 1494 by James IV. It is a handsome Gothic building, and is now divided into two separate places of worship, in connection with the Church of Scotland, denominated the 'East and West Churches'. The east church is allowed to be a very good, if not the best, specimen of Gothic architecture in Scotland. From the top of the tower a splendid view is obtained. Here the top of the tower a splendid view is obtained. Here the Regent Arran publicly renounced Popery in 1543, and James VI was crowned, while John Knox preached his sermon, in 1567, and his son Henry was baptized with great magnificence. A spire in Broad Street marks the Town House, in which a relic of old times, the Stirling Jug, or standard pint, similar to our Winchester measure, is kept. For several years it was lost, but was at length discovered by the sagacity of the late Dr Bryce, in the corner of a garret of a Jacobite brazier. Here also are the keys of the old bridge, which was partly destroyed in 1745, to cut off the retreat of Charles Stuart; likewise the keys of the port gates of the burgh, Stirling being at one time a walled town, much of which still remains. About 1 ½ mile up the river is the site where Kildean Bridge stood, the place where Wallace defeated the English in 1207. The railway crosses the Forth at Stirling. The old bridge is within a few hundred yards, but the old wooden bridge of the days of Wallace, which stood about 1 ½ mile up the river at Kildean, has long ago disappeared. The junction of the Forth & Clyde Railway is at Stirling, from whence tourists may reach Loch Lomond in 1 ½ hours.

Here are various literary and benevolent institutes. The Athenaeum and Library, in King Street, with a clock spire. Cowan's Hospital, near the church, founded in 1633, possesses an income of more than £3,000; and the founder's statue. Another hospital exists for the relief of the burgesses. Drummond's Museum of agricultural implements, &c., should be visited; it is 160 feet long.

Excursions from Stirling to Loch Katrine, &c. The best companion for this trip is the *Lady of the Lake*. The distances are – to Doune, 9 miles; Callander, 8 miles; Collantogle Ford, 3 miles; Bridge of Turk, 5 miles; Trossachs, 3 miles; Loch

Katrine and Inversnaid, on Loch Lomond, 12 miles; about 40 miles altogether, or 80 round to Glasgow – but this portion includes steam and railway. At Doune, on the Teith, is an old castle of the Stuarts. Callander, where the pass of Leny turns up Strathire and Loch Lubnaig. Ben Ledi in view, 3,000 feet high. From Ben Ledi was seen the cross of fire. Lord John Russell spent the summer of 1858 here, when he was made a freeman of Stirling, and addressed the burgesses on the Duke of Welligton's death. At Collantogle Ford, on the Teith, Fitz-James defeated Rhoderic Dhu, and began his celebrated ride to Stirling. Loch Vennachar, three miles long, and its banks well wooded. Bridge of Turk, at the bottom of Loch Achray, and the mouth of Glenfinglas. Aberfoyle, on the Forth, is four or five miles to the south (see *Rob Roy*). The naked top of Ben An to the right Trossachs, a wild rugged pass of a mile, between Loch Achray and Loch Katrine (i.e. Cateran, a thief), the lake of Scott's poem. 'High on the south' is 'huge Benvenue,' 2,800 feet high, in the district of Menteith. Lochs Ard and Awe are in this direction, but the regular road is on the north side of the lake, to the ferry, the top of which is seven miles. Ponies may be had hence to Loch Lomond, which is descended by steamer. To Airthrie Wells and Bridge of Allan, a beautiful place of resort on the Allan. Dunblane, on the Porth road, was once the bishopric of the excellent Archbishop Leighton; the Cathedral Church is of the 12th century. Sheriff's Muir, where the Duke of Argyll and Marr fought a drawn battle in 1715, is near. It is said that the Duke was a better Christian than a soldier on this occasion, as he would not let his right hand know what his left hand had done. The river Devon rises here; Allan may be followed to its crook or bend, and the three falls at Caldron Lynn. Ben Cleuch or Ben Buck, in the Ochils, is 2,420 ft. high. Demyatt, near Logie, is 1,345 feet high; a famous view. Up the Forth (10 miles), Port of Monteith, and Aberfoyle (20 miles from Stirling). To the south of Stirling the rail traverses a wide plain, on which several battles have been fought, viz.: Bannockburn (1314), near St Ninian's, a great place for nailers, &c.; Sauchieburn (1488, James III killed); Falkirk (1288, Wallace defeated). The last is famous for its cattle fair, and is near the Carron Iron Works. Kilsyth, where Baillie was beaten by Montrose (1645). This is near Castlecary, and other remnants of the Antonine Wall, locally called Graham's Dyke.

For continuation of this route to Perth, Aberdeen, and Inverness, see page 83.

## FORTH AND CLYDE JUNCTION
### Stirling to Balloch and Loch Lomond

This is a short line of thirty miles, connecting the eastern counties with the West Highlands of Scotland. It commences at Stirling, and passes in its route the stations of GARGUNNOCK, KIPPEN, PORT OF MONTEITH, BUCKLIVIE, BALFRON, GARTNESS, DRYMEN, KILMARONOCK, and JAMESTOWN, connecting itself with the Dumbartonshire Railway at BALLOCH.

*Clockwise from top left:* Cowane's Hospital, also known as the Guild Hall, Stirling.

The Martyr's Monument to two Covenanters who were drowned in Wigtownshire in 1685.

Caledonian Railway poster from *c.* 1921.

Stirling's King Stret with the Athenaeum at the top.

The highlands occupy about two-thirds of the nature of this county, which returns one member; the lowlands are situated on the eastern and southern extremities, which contain some of the richest land in Great Britain; and to the west, where the Grampians first rise, for almost the whole breadth of the country, the high grounds are penetrated by straths and glens of considerable extent, each traversed by its own streams, and diversified by numerous lakes. Several of the mountains in this district are upwards of three thousand feet high, the highest being Ben Lawers, on the west side of Loch Tay, Benmore, on the south-west, and Sohchallion, on the north-east. The most considerable lakes are Loch Tay, in the centre of the Highland district, about fifteen miles long and one broad, with a depth varying from fifteen to a hundred fathoms; Loch Ericht on the north-west, extending into Invernessshire, is still longer, but not so broad; Loch Rannoch, south-east of the former, twelve miles long; Loch Earn, south from Loch Tay; and Lochs Vennachar, Achray, and Katrine, on the south-west.

Stirling to Crieff Junction

BRIDGE OF ALLAN

A telegraph station.

HOTELS – Royal; Queen

BRIDGE OF ALLAN is denominated the Queen of Scottish watering places, and is a place of great resort in summer. It is also much frequented in winter by invalids, on account of the salubrity of its climate. There are several places of worship, and good medical advice. The river Allan runs through the village, in which tolerable trout fishing may be had. The river Teith, a much larger stream, is within an hour's walk. Loch Ard, and other lochs, famous for trout fishing, are easy of access. There are mineral springs close to the village, pronounced by high authority to possess strong purgative qualities. Kippenross, the seat of J. Stirling, Esq., famous for its large plane tree, 42 feet in circumference, and 470 years old, is near at hand.

DUNBLANE

Telegraph station at Bridge of Allan, 2 miles.

HOTEL – Dewar's

MARKET DAY – Thursday

FAIRS – 1st Wednesday in March, Tuesday after May 26th, August 10th, 1st Tuesday in November.

This city, though it has only a village population, is well worth visiting. The Cathedral is much admired, and in good preservation. It has a mineral spring, to which many visitors resort during the summer months. Tannahill's beautiful song

*Clockwise from top left:* An 1860s view of the Airthrey Mineral Well, Bridge of Allan. The Spa encouraged tourism to the area from the early Victorian age.

The Forth & Clyde Junction Railway engine shed at Stirling, with a Sentinel rail car inside.

Sherrifmuir Inn is close to the battlefield of Sherrifmuir, a 1715 Jacobite Rebellion site.

Greenloaning Inn, where Robert Burns stayed when he visited here.

The Kippenross Walk, Dunblane, with the railway crossing the river Allan.

of 'Jessie, the flower of Dunblane,' has given it popularity. The Allan runs through the village. A beautiful foot road by the river side runs between Dunblane and Bridge of Allan.

## DUNBLANE, DOUNE, AND CALLANDER
This line opens out a district full of interest to the tourist, and one which few will overlook who have an opportunity to visit these parts. From Dunblane the line takes a westerly direction, calling at the village of

## DOUNE
Telegraph station at Bridge of Allan
HOTEL – Macintyre's
This place is remarkable for its Castle, now in ruins, cresting the top of a lofty eminence, overlooking the Teith. Its noble founder is supposed to be Murdoch, Duke of Albany. It affords a fine opportunity for the ramber.

## CALLANDER
Telegraph station at Bridge of Allan
HOTEL – The Dreadnought
This place is perhaps most noted as being the centre of a most beautiful and highly picturesque district. It is the station for the Trossachs and Loch Katrine, and of course via Inversnaid to Loch Lomond and the western Highlands. There are several communications daily during the season by Coach, between this, the Trossachs, and Loch Katrine.

KINBUCK station.

## GREENLOANING
Telegraph station at Stirling, 11 miles.
MONEY ORDER OFFICE at Dunblane, 6 miles.

BLACKFORD and CRIEFF JUNCTION stations.

## CRIEFF
POPULATION about 3,824.
Telegraph station at Perth, 24 ½ miles.
HOTEL – Drummond Arms
MARKET DAY – Thursday
FAIRS – January 1st, 3rd Tuesday in June, October 1st for cattle.
This town contains a population of 4,333, who are employed in the cotton, linen, and general trade, and has a tollbooth, two churches, four chapels, news and assembly rooms, Masonic lodge, corn, flax, and other mills, distilleries,

THE FEUS, AUCHTERARDER.

High Street.

Perth.

*Clockwise from top left:*
Crieff High Street.

Auchterarder has one of Scotland's longest High Streets.

Scottish Central Railway No.7 at Perth, late 1850s. It was typical of locomotives of this period.

The High Street, Perth, *c.* 1905.

tanneries, dye works, St Margaret's Ladies' College, obelisk to Sir David Baird, 80 ½ feet high. The church was rebuilt in 1787, on the site of an old pointed one, and coins bearing Robert I were found. The west church was built by subscription. In the vicinity is Drummond Castle, the seat of Lady Willoughby d'Eresby.

Crieff Junction to Perth

## AUCHTERARDER

POPULATION about 2,620

Telegraph station at Perth, 13 ½ miles.

HOTEL – Star.

MARKET DAYS – Friday and Saturday

FAIRS – Last Tuesday in March, 1st Tuesday in May, December 6th, August, September, and October.

This place is famous for having given rise to the formation of the Free Church in 1843. At Aberuthven is the old church, remains of King Malcolm's hunting seat, and St Mungo's chapel.

DUNNING, FORTEVIOT, and FORGANDENNY stations

## PERTH

A telegraph station

HOTELS – Royal George; Salutation; Star

STEAMERS to and from Dundee, twice daily. Fare 1s 6d (2 ½ hours)

MARKET DAY – Friday

FAIRS – 1st Friday in March, July, and September 3rd Friday in October, 2nd Friday in December, and Tuesday after Inverness fair.

BANKERS – Perth Banking Company; Branch Bank of Scotland; British Linen Co., Central Bank of Scotland; Commercial and National Bank of Scotland.

The capital of Perthshire, which county returns one member, the middle of Scotland, a parliamentary burgh, and a port, to which steamers and small craft come up from the sea by the Firth of Tay. Population about 23,835, who return one member. Its situation, on the north and south inches, or meadows, of the Tay, is very beautiful. From the Monerieffs' seat, on a trap hill, to the south, 756 feet high, there are some of the most splendid views in Scotland, embracing the city, and the course of the river, from the Grampians to Dundee. Scott refers to it at the beginning of the 'Fair Maid of Perth.' When Agricola's Roman legions came in sight of the river, they saluted it with cries of Ecce Tiber! But it is hardly a compliment to compare this respectable stream with that now filthy but immortal ditch, the modern Tiber. One of Smeaton's bridges, 900 feet long, crosses the Tay; the greatest width of the Tiber is 200 feet. Both streams, however, are subject to heavy floods. The Romans founded a town here called Bertha. Some muslin, cotton, and silk goods are manufactured here, but the trade is not in a prosperous state.

*Top:* A North British Railway Atlantic 4-4-2 leave Perth station, *c.* 1905, heading south. Perth is a majo junction even today, with lines radiating to Aberdeer Inverness, Edinburgh and Glasgow.

*Above:* The last oak of Birnam, once part of a hug forest mentioned in Shakespeare's *Macbeth.*

*Left:* Hal o' the Wynd House, Perth, mentioned in *Th Fair Maid of Perth,* by Sir Walter Scott.

In the present day, Perth is the handsomest town, of its size, in Scotland, and in some respects resembles Edinburgh. It consists principally of two street, proceeding westward from the Tay, parallel to each other, and these are intersected, from north to south, by cross streets. In the High-street is the Guild Hall. At the north-east corner of the town the Tay is crossed by a bridge of ten arches. By far the most pleasing characteristics of Perth, in a popular point of view, are the two large meadows on the north and south sides of the town, which are exclusively appropriated for the recreation of the people.

In 1600 an attempt, or a pretended attempt, the history of which is not accurately settled, was made to seize the person of James I, under the name of the 'Gowrie Plot,' from the house in which he then resided. The site of this is now occupied by the County Buildings, built by Smirke, in the Grecian style; here are the County and Law Courts, with various pictures, one being Raeburn's portrait of Neil Gow:

> The man that play'd the fiddle weel,
> And dearly lo'ed the whisky O.

St John Baptist's Church, or Kirk, is in fact three churches, and is 270 feet long, with a spire 155 feet high. In the east kirk is the grave of James I (of Scotland), who was killed in the Blackfriars, in 1437; and a painted window. It was in an older church, on this site, that Knox preached with so much energy, in 1559, that the people sallied out to destroy the Romish monasteries, &c.; but their hearts were on fire from the cruelties of the mother of abominations, and the remembrance of six martyrs hung on the south inch, in front of the Spey Tower of the Greyfriary, in which Cardinal Beaton sat. This spot is now turned into gardens, and a cemetery; a gate only remains.

The Freemasons' Hall occupies the place of the old House (pulled down in 1818) and Castle, in which many Parliaments were held, till their meetings were transferred to Edinburgh, upon the death of James I. Scone Palace being then the usual residence of the Sovereign. He founded a Carthusian Friary, which James VI converted into a Hospital. This was rebuilt in 1750, the old one having been battered down along with the city cross by Cromwell in 1651. On this occasion he erected a fort to command the town, on the North Inch. Here is the race course, on which the celebrated combat took place, before Robert II, between Clan Chattan and Clan Kay, thirty on each side, which is so graphically described in Scott's 'Fair Maid of Perth.'

The Model Prison, for 350 prisoners, was used to confine French prisoners, in the revolutionary war. In 1832 a Public Library and Museum were erected in George-street, in compliment to Provost Marshall. A large Lunatic Asylum stands in the north suburbs, near Kinnoul and Dickson's Nursery. Both Inches, beyond the city bounds, are planted with trees, and laid out in beautiful walks.

NEIGHBOURHOOD OF PERTH – Kinfauns Castle (3 miles), Lord Gray's seat, contains the great Charteris sword, nearly 6 feet long – Charteris was the patron of Perth. Behind is Kinnoul Hill, a basalt ridge, at the termination of Siddaw Hills, 630 feet high; the view from it is magnificent. Errol House is three miles from this, on that rich and fertile tract of the Tay, called the 'Carse of Gowrie,' once covered by the river. Bridge of Eard, 5 miles south-east of Perth, is a pretty village, near the Picaithley sulphur waters. The Earn joins the Tay, a few miles lower down, past Abernethy (and its round tower); it may be ascended here, past Dupplin Castle, the Earl of Kinnoul's seat. The road to Crieff crosses Tippermuir, where Montrose routed the Covenanters in 1645. Huntingtoun, near it, now a cotton factory, belonged to the Gowries. Following this road you reach Crieff, in Strath-Earn, under a pass of the Grampians, 14 miles from Perth. Thence it is 13 miles to St Fillans, at the bottom of Loch Earn; which is surrounded by fine mountains, one of which, Ben Voirlich, is 3,050 feet high; then up the Loch and through Glen Dochart, &c., to the top of Loch Lomond, about 30 miles.

ASCENT OF THE TAY – It is about 20 miles to Dunkeld, and 20 more to Taymouth. Scone Palace, the seat of the Earl of Mansfield, is a handsome building, on the site of the royal palace in which Charles II and the Chevalier were crowned. This was once the seat of the Culdee, and here the famous Coronation Stone was kept, which originally came from Tara Hill in Ireland, and which Edward I carried off to Westminster Abbey where it is fixed under Edward the Confessor's Chair. The river Almond, from Glen Almond, now joins the Tay. At Luncarty Bleach Works (the spot where the Danes were defeated by Kenneth III and the Hays), the river turns off to the cast up the valley of Strathmore, passing over Campsiefall, near Cargill; and joins the road again near the celebrated Birnam Wood (on a hill, 1.580 feet high), the sight of which, in motion, filled Macbeth with despair.

| Sinward | What wood is this before us? |
|---|---|
| Monteith | The wood of Birnam |
| Malcolm | Let every soldier hew him down a bough |
| | And bear't before him; thereby shall we shade |
| | The number of our host, and make discovery |
| | Err in report of us |

*Macbeth* Act 5, Scene IV.

It was part of a royal forest. There is a noble view over the valley of the Tay; one of the opposite hills, to the south-east is Dunsinane, about 1,100 feet high, with some remains of the usurper's castle.

Scene V Dunsinane
Within the Castle – Enter Messenger
Mess.            Gracious, my lord!

|       | I shall report that which I say I saw, |
|-------|---------------------------------------|
|       | But know not how to do it. |
| Mac.  | Well, say sir. |
| Mess. | As I did stand my watch upon the hill, |
|       | I looked towards Birnam, and anon, methought |
|       | The wood began to move. |
| Mac.  | If thou speakest false, |
|       | Upon the next tree shalt thou hang alive, |
|       | Till famine cling thee; if thy speech be sooth |
|       | I care not if thou do for me as much. |
|       | I pall in resolution, and begin |
|       | To doubt the equivocation of the fiend |
|       | That lies like truth: Fear not, till Birnam Wood |
|       | Do come to Dunsinane. And now a wood |
|       | Comes toward Dunsinane. Arm, arm, and out! |

According to some accounts Macbeth escaped from the field of battle and fled up the vale of Strathmore, and was killed at Lumphanan, near Kincardine O'Neil. Dunkeld. Logierait, 8 miles further; here the Tummel, fed by various mountain streams from the Grampians, joins the Tay; most of these feeders unite in the Garry, which comes down the Inverness road, receives the Tilt from Glen-tilt (on the way to Braemar,) and falls into the Tummel by the pass of Killiecrankie, where Claverhouse fell in 1680. From Logierait up they Tay, past Grandtully, Murthly, Castle Menzies, &c., to Taymouth, the Marquis of Breadalbane's seat. The scenery is truly beautiful. Up Loch Tay (15 miles long) through Glen Dochart, &c., to the head of Loch Lomond, is 45 miles.

## PERTH, ALMOND VALLEY, & METHVEN
### Perth to Methven

This is a line about six miles long, passing through ALMOND BANK, to

## METHVEN

Here is Methven Castle, within the grounds of which is the Pepperwell Oak, the trunk of which is eighteen feet in circumference. In this neighbourhood Robert Bruce was defeated, June 19th, 1306, by the English, under the command of the Earl of Pembroke.

*Clockwise from top left:* The pleasure steamer Shamrock, near Perth. Below is Dundee Harbour with whalers drying sails. A Caledonian 4-4-0 steams past Magdalen Green. Left is a Caledonian Cardean-class 4-6-0 at Dundee on the express to Aberdeen via Forfar.

WEST COAST CORRIDOR EXPRESS AT DUNDEE.

# Dundee, Perth & Aberdeen

Passing KINFAUNS (near which is Kinfauns Castle) and GLENCARSE (close to which is the seat of C. Hunter, Esq.), we reach ERROL, INCHTURE, and LONGFORGAN stations. At the latter is a church, rebuilt in the pointed style in 1795, and near which in 1790, 300 coins of Edward I's reign were found. In the vicinity are Drummie, Lord Kinnaird, and Myterefield, T. White, Esq.

Passing INVERGOWRIE station, we arrive at

## DUNDEE

A telegraph station.

HOTELS – Royal, British, Crown.

MARKET DAYS – Tuesday and Friday

FAIRS – Tuesday after July 11th, August 26th, and September 19th.

BANKERS – British Linen Co.; Dundee Banking Co.; Bank of Scotland; National Bank of Scotland; East Bank of Scotland.

The capital of Forfarshire, seat of the Scottish linen trade, a port and burgh (returning one member), with a population of about 78,931, situated on the north side of the Tay. Coming direct from the metropolis, a ferry of two miles must be crossed, from Broughty to Tay Port, in connexion with the railway. A swelling hill behind the town, called Dundee Law, is 525 feet high to the camp on the top. Here Montrose sat while his troops sacked the town, in 1645, after the battle of Tippermuir. Since 1815, Dundee has been greatly improved by the new quays, wet and graving docks, and the deepening of the chief harbour. About 50,000 tons of shipping belong to the port, a small portion being engaged in the whale fisheries. The factories for spinning and weaving flax exceed 100, employing as many as 16,000 hands, three-fourths of whom are women. Coarse linens, osnaburghs, diapers, sail-cloth, rope, canvas, &c., are the chief goods made up.

Near the harbour is the triumphal arch, 82 feet wide, built on the occasion of the Queen's visit in 1844. Among the modern improvements which have taken place in Dundee, may be noticed those in Union Street, which opens a communication with the Craig pier and the Nethergate; indeed, nearly all the old buildings have been superseded by new ones. In front of the quay, along the margin of the Tay, are the various docks and shipyards, terminated on the west by the Craig Pier, which is exclusively used for the large ferry steam-boats. On the east the piers project into the deep water, on which are placed various coloured lights to guide the seamen after sunset. Opposite the town is a beacon, which is built on a dangerous rock. Nearly the whole of the space now appropriated to the docks, was originally a semicircular sandy beach, but by great exertion the spirit inhabitants have erected a series of quays which are unequalled in Scotland. There are 20 churches and chapels. Three churches stand together on the site of that founded by William the Lion's brother, David (the hero of Scott's *Talisman*) in pursuance of a vow made at sea on returning from the Crusades; its square tower, 156 feet high, still remains, though damaged by a fierce storm in 1840. David also built a castle, which figures in the war of independence as having been taken by Wallace and Bruce. The former great patriot was educated at the priory in this town, and made himself known, about 1271, by killing Delly, an insolent young Norman knight in the Governor's train. The Town House in High Street, was built by Adams, in 1734; other buildings are, the Exchange, Trades Hall, Academy, St. Andrew's Church, with a tall spire, &c.

Some of the oldest houses are in Seagate. High Street and Murraygate are the most bustling thoroughfares. When Charles II was crowned at Scone in 1650, by the Covenanters, he came to reside at Whitehall, in the Nethergate, since pulled down. Another house, in the middle of High Street, was occupied by Monk (after taking the town by storm in 1645); and by the Pretender, in 1716; it was also the birthplace of Monmouth's widow, Anne, Duchess of Buccleugh (the Lady of Brankxholme Tower, in the 'Lay of the Last Minstre.' In the Cowgate is an arch from which Wishart, the martyr, preached during the plague of 1544, the infected part of his congregation being kept by themselves on one side. Towards Dundee Law, at the end of Dunhope Wynd, is Dunhope Castle (now a barrack), which belonged to the Scrymgeours, (hereditary standard-bearers of Scotland), and to the famous Graham of Claverhouse, whom James II created Viscount Dundee, before his death at Killiecrankie. Mackenzie, the great lawyer, and Ivory, one of the first mathematicians of modern days, were natives of Dundee, a name supposed to be derived from Donum-Dei or, God-given, applied to it by David, its founder.

Within a short distance are, Broughty Castle; Gray the seat of Lord Gray; Camperdown, that of Lord Duncan; and Mains, another of Claverhouse's seats.

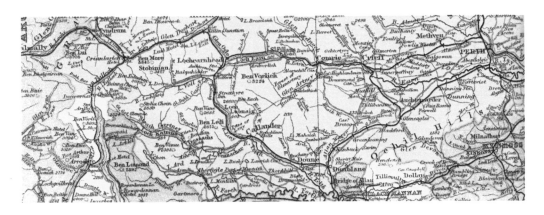

# Inverness & Aberdeen Jcn

INVERNESS & ABERDEEN JUNCTION
Keith to Inverness and Invergordon

By means of this line there is now an unbroken connection between Aberdeen and Invergordon. Continuing our journey from Keith, we pass the station of MULBEN, and arrive at

ORTON

The Morayshire Railway here diverges to the left. It takes a direction parallel with the river, and through the valley of the Spey. It passes the stations of ROTHES, CRAIGELLACHIE, and STRATHSPEY, which gives name to a Highland dance, and the junction of a short branch to DUFFTOWN, ABERLOUR, CARRON, BLACKBOAT, BALLINDALLOCH, ADVIE, DALVIE, CROMDALE, and GRANTOWN, to ABERNETHY.

Leaving Orton, onward, we pass FOCHABERS and LEANBRYDE, and arrive at

ELGIN

A telegraph station.

HOTEL – Gordon Arms; Star Inn (called Devies' Hotel).

MARKET DAYS – Tuesday and Friday.

FAIRS – 3rd Friday in February, March, and April, 2nd Friday in May, 1st Tuesday in June, 3rd Tuesday in July, August, September, and October, 3rd Wednesday in December.

This town has a population of about 7,277, who return one member – the county another, and was founded by Helgy, a Norwegian. It is situated 5 miles from the sea, on the river Lossie, and contains 5 chapels, prison, library, news and assembly rooms, literary and horticultural societies, breweries, gas and water-works, woollen factory, grammar school, free school, hospital school of industry, founded by General Anderson (a native who was a poor boy of this town), on the site of Bishop Andrew's Domus Dei, erected in 1227; hospital founded by Dr Gray, a native, and built by Gillespie; pauper lunatic asylum, church in the Grecian style. The cathedral was built in the latter part of the 14th century, and is one of the finest specimens in Scotland of the first pointed style of architecture. Its extreme length is 289 feet, the breadth of nave and side aisles, 87 feet. The original building was completed in 1242, but was destroyed by the 'Wolfe of Badenoch' in 1390 (vide Sir T. Dick Lander's 'Wolfe of Badenoch'). The present building, through lack of funds, was not completed till 1506. 'Mighty, though in ruins,' the western towers are 84 feet high, and the eastern turrets 64 feet. Near the south gate is the stone coffin of King Duncan, who was subsequently reinterred at Icolmkill (see Iona, page 63). The apprentice's aisle, octagonal chapter house, the tombs of Bishops Innes and Dunbas, and the lavatory where Marjory Gilgean lived, are worthy of special attention.

In the vicinity is Pluscarden Abbey, one of the finest specimens of Gothic architecture in the North of Scotland. Although much overgrown with ivy, the interior is fine, and contains the remains of some fine frescoes.

From Elgin a short branch of six miles turns off to the right to

## LOSSIEMOUTH (Branch)
Telegraph station at Elgin, 6 miles.
HOTEL – Railway.
STEAMERS to and from Aberdeen, Edinburgh, Inverness, &c.
Here lead with silver is found to the west in the quartz.

Retracing our steps to Elgin, and again proceeding onward, we come to the station of ALVES, the junction of a short line to BURGHEAD, a small bathing place, at the entrance to the Moray Firth. Fishing forms a considerable item in its commerce.

KINLOSS (the junction of a line, three miles long, to the town of FINDHORN).

FORRES – Here is Forres Castle, on the heath where Macbeth met the Weird Sisters, and murdered Banquo; there is also Sweno's Pillar, an ancient carved stone, 20 feet high, commemorating a treaty with the Danes.

BRODIE station.

## NAIRN
A telegraph station.
HOTEL – Anderson's.
MARKET DAYS – Tuesday, Thursday, and Friday.
FAIRS – April 2nd, June 19th, August 13th, September 4th, October 3rd, and November 1st.

The Brighton of the North, a favourite sea bathing place, and the county town of Nairnshire. It contains three kirks (Established, Free Kirk, and U.P.), an Episcopal Chapel (St Columa's), schools, new museum, court house, gaol, new pier (1860), and bridge, gas and water works, and baths. The beach is sandy, and the excellent bathing machines are in great requisition. The 'Links' is a favourite promenade, on which a handsome hotel was erected in 1859. It gives the title of Baroness to Lady Keith. Excellent salmon and trout fisheries are close at hand.

Seven and a half miles from Nairn is Kilravock (pronounced Kilrauch) Castle, the property of Colonel Rose, and Contray, H. Davidson.

## CAWDOR

Here is Cawdor Castle, the seat of Lord Cawdor built in 1400, on the site of that which belonged to Macbeth, 'The Thane of Cawdor.' There is a curious drawbridge and portcullis; and the Castle contains some old tapestry, secret passages, a vault under the tower, in which is an ancient tree, where 'success to the hawthorn' (house of Cawdor) is drunk by the peasantry. King Duncan is reported to have been murdered here. The 'Burn' of Cawdor is one of the most beautiful in Scotland; it is a miniature Rhine without the towns and vineyards, and is well worth a visit from those who can realise that

> Many a grace is beaming
> O'er the burn, the wishing brook

## FORT GEORGE

This fort, erected in 1746, covers 10 acres, and holds a small garrison. There is a ferry here across the firth, on the opposite side of which (in Rossshire) is Fortrose, once the seat of the Bishop of Ross; the remains of the old abbey still exist. Further east about 1 ½ mile, is Rosemarkie, and 3 miles further, the Burn of Ethie, hwere Hugh Miller's geological discoveries were made.

Further on we reach DALCROSS, the castle at which has an old tower of the Clan Chattan, and just beyond is

## CULLODEN

Not far from which is Culloden Moor, where Charles Stuart was defeated by the Duke of Cumberland, in May, 1746 (who laid out Virginia water, near Windsor), and Culloden House, seat of C. Mackinnon, Esq., at which Prince Charles lodged the night before the battle, and left his stick. The remains of the cairn where the Duke stood lie close to the road. The moor has latterly been brought partly under cultivation. A little to the east of the moor, on the other side of the river Nairn, lies

Clava, at which are a number of Druidical remains, happily saved from the grasping hand of a Highland laird. They are most interesting, but can oly be reached on foot. They consist of cairns and circles, and are the most perfect remains of the kind in Scotland. They were saved from destruction by a young Englishman, who brought the matter before the Scottish Society of Antiquarians. Other less important Druidical remains lie between Dalcross Castle and Inverness.

## INVERNESS-SHIRE

This is one of the largest counties of Scotland, and returns one member. Its surface is in general extremely ragged and uneven, consisting of vast ranges of mountains, separated from each other by narrow and deep vallies. These

*Clockwise from top left:* One of the cairns at Clava. Next is the wharf at Muirtown on the Caledonian Canal. Below is Elgin railway station, a junction with the LNER. Bottom right is Forres station, with the Highland Railway's *Ben Dearg* ready to depart. Bottom left is Fort George, a Jacobite period barracks, during sports day in the early 1900s. Above is Fort George station. At the time of *Bradshaw's Guide*, this was pretty much as far north as the railways reached. There was no far north line to Thurso, and no line to Kyle of Lochalsh. The railway reached Dingwall. The 1860s saw the rump of the network but the following fifty years saw huge changes too. as the network grew to cover the Highlands.

mountains stretch across the whole country, from one end of the island to another, and lie parallel to every valley, rising like immense walls on both sides while the intersected country sinks deep between the, with a lake, or rapid river, or an arm of the sea, following in the centre. No sooner is one defile passed over than a second range of hills comes into view, which contains another, and a strath of uninhabited country. The great Caledonian Glen, which runs in a straight line nearly north-east and south-west, divides the county into two almost equal parts. This valley, in the greater part of its length, is naturally filled with water, and forms a long chain of lakes succeeding each other – a circumstance which suggested the idea of transferring the whole into the Caledonian Canal.

## INVERNESS

A telegraph station.

HOTELS – The Railway; Caledonian, Church Street; Union, High Street.

BANKERS – British Linen Co.; Bank of Scotland; Caledonian Commercial Bank of Scotland; National Bank of Scotland; North of Scotland.

Inverness, with a population of about 12,793, who return one member, lies at the foot of the Northern Highlands, on the Moray Firth, where the Caledonian Canal terminates, 106 miles from Aberdeen. The mouth of the Firth is guarded by Fort George and Fortrose, where Sir J. Mackintosh went to school. A small river, called the Ness, opening into a little estuary, or Inver, in Gaelic, gives name to the town, which is situated among plantations, and modern hills, fertile and cultivated. Small ships are able to unload at Kessock Ferry, which divides the Firth from Loch Beauty. Inverness lies as it were a tthe back of Scotland, in a part formerly little visited or accessible. About the year 1770, it had no banks, lamps, or tiled houses, and one cargo of coal called 'blackstones') a year was enough to supply the demand; but smuggled tea, brandy, fish, and game were plentiful. It was not too far north for Cromwell, who paid it a visit in 1651, and built a fort; and it was occupied about a century later by Charles Stuart and the Duke of Cumberland, both of whom had their quarters at the Drummuirs' house in Church Street, then the best one in the town. At present it contains several well built streets and houses, among which are the Court House, on the site of a castle, built by the Thanes of Cawdor; Tolbooth or prison, with a spire, and a stone called Ciach-na-Cudden in front of it; twelve churches and chapels; six banks, besides Assembly Rooms, an Athenaeum, and a well-endowed Academy. There is a pleasant walk by the river, which rose so high in the great floods of 1849 as to break down the old stone bridge. The Episcopalian chapels are situated, one in Church street, and the other (the Bishop of Moray's) by the Ness. Manufactures, worsted stockings, tartans, brogues, and other essentially Highland productions. Invernessians speak purer English than any other Scotch people.

In the neighbourhood are various cairns and Druid's stones; Craid Phadric (or Patrick's Stone) Mountain, 1,150 feet high, with a vitrified fort on the top, cemented together by melting the surgace of the stone; Dochfour, seat of E. Baillie, Esq., near Dochfour Loch, and the Roman station of Romairie, not far from Loch Ness. At the top of Loch Beauly is the seat of Lord Lovat (the head of the Frasers), and remains of a priory where the Frasers and Chisholms are buried. Ellan-agash in Strath-Glass, is a pretty sheltered spot, which Sir Robert Peel bought for a Highland seat a little before his death.

The road to Perth leads up Strath-Spey, and through a pass of the Grampians. To the left of the road, three miles from Inverness, is the Culloden Cairn, a pile 100 feet high, in the midst of the desolate moor. It is traversed by the Nairn river; descending which you pass Cawdor Castle and Rait Castle.

Good roads made by the Government and the landholders strike through the Highlands in various directions, in the counties of Inverness, Ross, and Sutherland; fir timber, deer, game, and sheep are the chief products. Vast tracts are preserved for deer-stalking, while (in Sutherland especially) thousands of clansmen have been transplanted to Canada, to make room for sheep-farms. The narrow passages between he mountains are called Glens, the wider valleys are Straths, each being watered by its own stream, and the character of the scenery resembles that of Wales, with a more piercing mist, keener air, more lakes, and a more broken coast. Some of the highest peaks are 3,000 to 4,000 feet high. The coach road to the north runs near the coast past Dingwall, Bonar Bridge, Luing to Tongue, 88 miles; or to Tain, Dornoch, and Wick, 123 miles.

From Inverness to Fort William is 61 miles by coach, the road running close to the Caledonian Canal, which is traversed by steamers on the return trip to Glasgow, through Loch Ness, Lochy, &c. On the west side of Loch Ness are Glens Urquhart and Moriston, two of the finest in the Highlands, with Mealfourvonie between them, a mountain 2,730 feet high, opposite the magnificent Falls of Foyers. From Fort Augustus (about half-way) you may turn up Glengarry to Glenelg and Kyle, where there is a ferry over the Sound of Sleat to Skye; or you may visit the heads of the Spey, and the Parallel Roads of Glenroy, in Lochaber. At Fort William there are Ben Nevis, Lochiel, and Prince Charles's Monument (the spot where he hoisted his standard in 1745), and the fine views at Cam-na-Gaul Bay, near Corran Ferry. The county returns one member.

From Inverness the line proceeds northward, via BUNCHREW, LENTRAN, BEAULY, MUIR of ORD, and CONON, to

## DINGWALL

The county town of Ross, and a parliamentary borough, prettily situated about 5 miles to the south of Ben Wyvis and at the south west corner of the Cromarty Firth. This splendid estuary is 12 miles long, and 2 miles broad, and forms a magnificent harbour and place of refuge for vessels in stormy weather. The town carries on a trade with Edinburgh, and even London. It has a pillar, 57 feet high, erected to the memory of one of the Earls of Cromarty.

FOWLIS, NOVAR, and ALNESS stations.

## INVERGORDON

A village situated on the northerly side of Cromarty Firth. It has a good harbour, and is about 5 miles from the Light-house, which stands on West Sutor, a bold and rocky eminence at the entrance to the Firth.